WE HAVE
OVERCOME

WE HAVE
OVERCOME

AN IMMIGRANT'S LETTER TO
THE AMERICAN PEOPLE

JASON D. HILL

A BOMBARDIER BOOKS BOOK
An Imprint of Post Hill Press

We Have Overcome:
An Immigrant's Letter to the American People
© 2018 by Jason D. Hill
All Rights Reserved

ISBN: 978-1-68261-730-4
ISBN (eBook): 978-1-68261-731-1

Cover Photography by Monika Łozińska.
Cover Design by Tricia Principe, principedesign.com

The idea for *We Have Overcome* is based on an article in the October 2017 issue of *Commentary*.

BOMBARDIER
BOOKS

Post Hill Press
New York • Nashville
posthillpress.com

Printed in the United States of America

To the American People
in the name of the best within you.

Contents

My Fellow Americans

W E LIVE IN AN ERA of deep resentment, envy, and hatred of our great and noble nation. It has become fashionable within certain circles in the United States of America to malign our republic as an imperialist, racist, and white supremacist country that exploits its racial minorities and keeps them outside the pantheon of the human community and the domain of the ethical.

Our celebrated writers and intellectuals pen books that receive accolades by critics who claim that America is ruled by majoritarian pigs, and that the American dream is the nefarious fabrication of white racists who have used it to exploit blacks. Some have claimed that the concept of The Dream itself is false, and that it is predicated on a specious hope that ought to be rejected by all Americans, but, more specifically, by black Americans.

We live in the age of militant *Americaphobia!*

We live in an era when the most benevolent and moral country on earth, along with her exceptional people with their amazing optimism, cheerfulness, and can-do forthrightness, are resented as crass, shoddy, xenophobic, and in inevitable decline. Americans as a group of people are good people. But, hatred of the good for being the good, hatred for the best and noblest of virtues that reside within you, has become a fashionable emotion among certain elitist groups who resent America and her people for such virtues. They resent America for the values forged in the crucibles of an unprecedented nation-state that has been a haven and a blessing for the talented, the strong, and the exceptional, but also for the poor, the benighted, the oppressed, the disenfranchised, and the dispossessed. This country could only have been such a haven because you, the American people, the most non-xenophobic and tolerant people in the world, have opened your home to the stranger and the foreigner time and time again. You have not forced the foreigner to make a self-abnegating Faustian bargain with his or her new country in the name of renouncing all roots and ancestral ties. You have only demanded that he or she pledge a thin and minimal political commitment to our great republic.

You have only required that that allegiance take precedence over tribal loyalties. This is why an America in the 21st century is one essentially free of racial, ethnical, and religious clashes and violence among all her varied peoples.

These detractors of America despise the fact that America, in a fundamental sense, is like the emotion of love itself: It is a command to rise. Like the human soul, America is a moral phenomenon. These haters are the original incompetents and lazy nonachievers who would seek to reduce all around them to the lowest common denominator within themselves. These privileged haters are range-of-the moment, concrete-bound primitives who have never known what it is to yearn for that most American of identities—not an ethnic or racial one, but an aspirational one. It is an identity belonging to any man, woman, or child who longs to suffuse the world with an original assemblage of who he or she is. We, the continuously aspiring human beings, whether we are Americans, or Americans-in-the-making, hear and respond to the quintessential elegiac American voice. It is an enticing one, at once soothing and inspiring, and it says: *I am an open canvas. Write and enact your script on me. Without you and your story and your narrative, the story of America is incomplete. This is America, where you can suffuse the nation's vast landscape with who you are and partake in a dialogue of national becoming.*

By constitutional design, America is a place of universal belonging. It is the prototype of what a benevolent universe looks like because it is the first country, and, *a fortiori*, a phenomenal social experiment that explicitly rejects lineage and blood as criteria for membership and belonging. It celebrates civic nationalism in place of ethnic or cultural nationalism as the political principle that would forge a common identity among strangers and foreigners from disparate parts of the globe.

You, the exceptional First People of this exceptional First Nation among all nations, you the co-creators of this, the most self-critical and reformed society on the face of the earth, have made these superlative achievements possible. The creation of your country and civilization is both a stupendous stylized work of art, as well as a work in scientific precision. Its sustainability and its inexorable progress over time are unmatched and unprecedented in the history of humanity.

When I try to tell detractors that the American Dream is a constitutive feature of America itself, made possible by the unbreakable spirit of the American people, they shore up a nefarious form of factionalism and appeal to an insidious cottage-industry of victimology often predicated on black suffering and white guilt, guilt for past transgressions that whites have long atoned for as a group. The detractors keep telling me that I am complicit in a beguiling narrative that hides a form of structural oppression against certain racial groups that forever keeps them outside the ambit of the American Dream and relegates them to an existential wasteland and eternal metaphysical anguish. This wasteland deliberately alienates blacks and other minorities from their own creative agency and renders them impotent against a system stacked against them from birth. I adduce my own life as evidence of the utter nonsense of this narrative. I am further told that I am either a fool or a deliberate player in the white supremacist construct that is a constitutive feature of American life and identity. I resist by stating that the current progressive nature of racial politics at work here in America proves that the United States is not, at this time, a white supremacist society because it does not have an official ideology of the supremacy of the white race as it once did. There are no laws explicitly preferring whites, or exclusionary or punitive of nonwhites simply on the grounds of race.

I am told off explicitly and given sundry journalistic minutiae ranging from fringe groups proclaiming the unassailability of white power, to lunatic psychotics who intermittently wage a spate of battles against blacks and other people of color. These are tragic occurrences that should arouse the anguish, anger, and indignation of all Americans, white, black, yellow, and all the shades in between. I sense a higher truth about my beloved adopted country, something that does not reside in any politician or in any administration that might be in power at the moment, something that transcends the pettiness of everyday life and the prejudices of cadres of individuals of many different groups. I sense a spirit, a *Geist* to the nation I love and the people whom I've decided, after having traveled all over the world, are my favorite people in the whole world. Who are these people, the American people? What is the fundamental nature of this country and its profound moral meaning? How has my life as a black immigrant been shaped (or not) by the racial politics of the nation I have called home for the past thirty-two years?

What is the truth about the nature of race and racial politics in this country I love that these detractors would shame me for loving? Why have some such as myself, an immigrant from Jamaica, along with countless other immigrants and a significant number of blacks who have been born and raised in America, been able to achieve some modicum of success, and others, only superlative achievements? Why were others thought to be inevitably barred from The Dream simply by virtue of their race and by insuperable barriers erected by a racial superstructure and its vanguards? If such were the case, did these white vanguards owe anything at all to the black individuals whose sufferings and hopelessness the detractors brandished as evidence of the utter irrefutability of an oppressive America? Did the individuals who failed within the system, and who were held up as certified moral icons of innocence and victimization, constitute a group that contained certain pathological features that ran either concurrently or independently to the system that had structurally stymied their existence and prevented them from flourishing? Was it the white vanguards who were responsible for the two-thirds of blacks born to unwed mothers and whose births have largely condemned them to a life of poverty? Was it the white vanguards who have been responsible for the disproportionate number of murders committed by black men that resulted in mass incarcerations that have blithely been referred to as evidence of a new form of Jim Crow in America? Mass incarcerations of people who commit crimes should not be referred to as racism. Its proper appellation is: justice.

Why have I never in my life in this country been disappointed by it? And, why, in spite of racial resistance from time to time—often and mostly from the detractors themselves who identified as progressives and radicals for a better world—have I never sought to actively fight racism, but have simply adduced myself as evidence of its irrationality?

But the biggest question and challenge and truth about race in America came to me as a shock and a deep psychological relief, one that left me with hope. As a black man living in America and studying her past very carefully, I came to see that race, while always endemic to America, was never metaphysically relevant to the true moral meaning of America. In fact, the very concept of race itself is a deep betrayal of the identity of the fundamental moral nature of the United States of America. I know this is a controversial position to hold. But, in the ensuing pages, I shall explain it as carefully as I can, explain what I believe is the true magnificent moral meaning of America, and explain why racial injustice is and has always been a betrayal of it. It is for this reason that I believe with all my heart that we have and will continue to make racial progress in this country, and that, one day, this noble and magnificent country will be a truly great cosmopolitan and color-blind society.

My convictions about America can be found by retracing my perceptions and analysis of the nation through my intimate experiences with its people. My convictions would be forged by witnessing the lives of, as well as the character traits of, other immigrants, most from humble origins, and those of black Americans who had embraced The Dream and faced the head-on challenges required for succeeding in America. My ideas about the moral meaning of America were derived from studying the history of the country itself. Later in my journey, in discovering the moral meaning of

America, I came to understand as an academic philosopher that it was in our institutions of higher learning,
our universities, that the real destruction of America was
taking place. Our nation's universities, in their advocacy
of *Americaphobia*, are not only sites of national security
threats, they are purveyors and repositories of racial divi-
siveness in this country. The biggest breach in this country
is not between blacks and whites. It is between the intellectuals and the people.

There is a formula for success in this great nation. I, as
well as others, have discovered it and applied it to our lives.
In this process, as people of color, we have discovered the
irrefutable metaphysical irrelevance of race in the United
States of America as it applies to *our* lives. In essence, we
have overcome it and its binding hold against a march
toward inevitable achievement.

I remain convinced that until that sense of the psychological irrelevance of race is internalized, and, thus,
becomes part of one's schema for being in the world, that
one will be compromised not by so-called structural and
systemic racism, but, rather, by the psychic and determinis-
tic hindrances that inflate the importance of race at the cost
of an intransigent individualism, personal responsibility,
self-accountability, and the reach for a never-ending aspirational identity that is wedded to grit, rationality, honor,

determination, resilience, tenacity, self-cultivation, frugality, perseverance, and a healthy dose of emotional stoicism.

Here is my story and that excavation of the moral meaning of America, of race, of identity, and of the nature of the indefatigable spirit that cannot accept defeat, that can only dream the impossible dream and make it real.

In the Name of the Best Within Us

O n August 11, 1985, at the age of twenty, I boarded an Air Jamaica aircraft bound for Atlanta. Clutching the hand of my seventy-two-year-old grandmother a little nervously, I was headed for what I still believe to be the greatest country on earth: The United States of America. Armed with 120 dollars, big dreams for my life, and the love of my family, I blew a kiss to the throngs of onlookers in the old rundown wavers' gallery who were waving crazily at everybody and nobody in particular—a hangover from the old colonial era—and never once looked back.

I recall that day as being the first day of my true and authentic life. My glamorous grandmother was decked out in pearls, high heels, and a silk dress. Greeting the flight attendant at the door, she said, head thrown back and with a raspy laugh, "America, here we come." My thirty-nine-year-old mother, the most courageous woman I have ever known, had, along with my younger brother, preceded us on our journey. My mother had given up her career in banking on the island and decided to head to America alone with us to start from scratch with very little money in hand, and to make a new life. Why? Because America was the place where anything was possible.

My mother had decided that her two sons were too young to be embarking on such a journey by themselves. She needed to be there to make sure her boys had family close by. For someone who had established roots in her native homeland, this move on her part was considered by several members of her inner circle as downright foolish and reckless. Why give up your life and career to start from scratch in a strange country? I thought that by uprooting her life at her age, she was not only courageous, but morally formidable, as well. It took faith and confidence and, above all, an enduring belief in the possibilities and opportunities that are a part of America's core identity. My mother, like all immigrants, believed in America—both for herself and her two sons.

Four and a half hours later, I, a newly minted legal immigrant, but feeling like some strange nocturnal creature seeing light for the first time, shielded my face against the harsh sunlight of the Atlanta skies with one hand and, with the other, protectively shielded my grandmother's slightly perspiring neck—although, really, there was nothing to protect it from. I was in the United States of America. Home of the Dreamers. The most magnificent land of opportunities. I was here to make something of my life: a black man who had never met any philosophers or real novelists in his life, but who was determined to become a philosopher and write books in the field of ethics, political philosophy, and American foreign policy. (I knew nothing of the latter at the time.) A Dreamer eager to publish poems and novels about the Caribbean that Americans would come to love. A gay man escaping the toxicity of homophobia that is constitutive of Jamaican identity, and who knew that, one day, in America, he could find peace and true love with a person of his choice and be left alone. That he would make no demands of his new country except that others place no obstructions in his path towards the enhancement of his life. It was a land where he would expect no special treatment because, in an exceptional place and time, one can already write one's own history. My ideas, I decided on that aircraft, will one day be taught in colleges and universities. Later, I will tell you the extent to which that *willed decision* became reality, and why this is possible only in the United States of America.

Before that wide-body A300 aircraft made its final touchdown in Atlanta, something magical happened while I floated at thirty-two thousand feet above the ground. At some point during the initial descent, I closed my eyes and made a covenant with this new country I would call my permanent home. I promised that, in the name of the best within me, I would cultivate the noblest virtues in my character and use them as the only legitimate currency to purchase a life that would be worthy of an American. I made a covenant with my soon-to-be approaching country that in the name of the best and highest in me, I would seek faith in life's better possibilities. That there would be no obstacles that my indefatigable spirit could not overcome, and that there would be no prejudice that a philosophy of individualism, which characterized the very essence of who I was at my core, could not transcend. This covenant spoke to the stupendous achievements I vowed to accomplish by taking advantage of the plethora of opportunities that I knew would become available to me. Riding that majestic bird in the sky, I thought of my life in moral terms: this was a *moral contract* I was making with my new country. The best within me was a code of conduct that I would enact between myself and my future compatriots. It was an ethos of benevolence and goodwill that I would extend, and one that I expected to be reciprocated. The America I anticipated meeting, and the one I have come to know and love, is a country predicated on mutual exchange.

If you show Americans respect, courtesy, basic warmth, and benevolence, then the majority of them—you, the American people, black, white, brown, yellow, or red—will basically respond in kind. Americans, as I imagined them while riding high in the sky, would not be a formidable people, but would, rather, be purposeful, driven, optimistic, and ambitious, such as myself. Like me, they would expect no special favors from anyone. Each person's fate, like my own, would be in his or her own hands. In this covenant, I made a sacred decision never to give up the struggle to succeed; never to capitulate to cynicism and bitterness; never to see myself as anyone's victim; to ask for help as little as possible (if I asked for any at all); and to never to be thought I was owed anything by anyone except to be left alone to pursue my dreams and cultivate my values and moral character. Thirty-two years later, I have never had to modify the covenant in any essential way. Its fundamentals remain the same. They are rooted in a highly individuated man who is an intransigent and rugged individualist, and whose proper posture is an upright one.

* * *

The early years were thrillingly difficult. They were filled with promise, vitality, and exuberance. We lived in Stone Mountain, Georgia, which, in 1985, my black friends liked to remind me was Ku Klux Klan country. It didn't matter. It was like the Jamaican women in the 1920s who had integrated the New York garment industry. Upon observing signs that said, "Coloreds Need Not Apply," they simply marched in in droves and applied for seamstress jobs. So, too, my family and countless Caribbean families marched *en masse* into Stone Mountain, in Klan country, and bought homes, joined their churches, and introduced ourselves in utter fearlessness—and that was that. None of us ever missed a night's sleep. We moved there because large houses were comparatively cheap, resale values were high, and we had absolutely no fear of white people. That emotion was alien to all of us. I introduced myself to my neighbors and, like most Southerners then and now, they were polite and courteous—they practiced good manners. Some of them expressed a desire to visit Jamaica. All welcomed me to America.

I often wondered what possessed fifteen thousand people from the Caribbean to descend upon Atlanta in the mid-1980s and integrate into the nearly all-white neighborhoods. It was true. Back then, Stone Mountain was a disproportionately white community populated by several members of the Ku Klux Klan. When I told black friends that my family and dozens of other Caribbean families were living in Stone Mountain, they were genuinely concerned for my safety. Most blacks were living on the south side of Atlanta in predominantly black neighborhoods; they thought we might be verbally harassed, physically assaulted, or, by the more apocalyptically minded among my beloved friends, lynched. They asked why we had chosen to move there. Were you social activists bent on integrating into the neighborhood?

"No," I responded vehemently, recoiling instantly from the thought of being identified as such. But, as an afterthought, I did add, "We probably will, eventually, by default, integrate the town and drive all those Klans people out." This was, incidentally, exactly what happened. But, such was not our intention. A year after moving to Stone Mountain, while on a lunch break in a bank where I was working full-time as a credit card debt collector, I tried to explain the moral psychology of what I thought was our motivation to one of my black friends who kept pestering me. She thought the Caribbeans were moving in because they wanted to be white, and that, in some strange way, we were "sellouts," though she could not exactly define in what way. I had just about had it with this nonsense.

"Listen," I explained to her, "I am an individualist. And, most of the Caribbeans and Jamaicans I know who are moving into Stone Mountain are incorrigible individualists. We don't care about race. We never have, and we never will. Period. It's not that we have never been touched by race. Many of us, my parents and grandparents included, came from British colonies in which we were subjected to racial indignities by the English colonial system. That had its own system of racial- and class-based taxonomies and hierarchies predicated on a nefarious system of pigmentocracy."

I explained to her that an implacable ethos of unbridled individualism prevents Caribbeans from submitting to this internalized system of racialization. They despised and eschewed racial classifications, along with any form of racial solidarity and biological collectivism predicated on racial ancestry. In their adopted country—America— they would accept it not grudgingly (we *are* realists), but amusingly, and certainly not with any degree of internal identification. This was what allowed my maternal grandmother, born of a Jewish father and a Jamaican mother, to laugh uproariously at a banker who, upon opening her senior's bank account, referred to her as Afro-American. She laughed, nodded, and then I think looked at the poor woman as a functioning psychotic, a truly color-blind person—and that was all there was to it.

I explained to my friend that twenty years after the magnificent Third Founding of America in the form of the Civil Rights Movement, Jamaicans and other Caribbeans had correctly made the assessment that America was the best place in the word for aspiring black immigrants to exist, and that in 1985, Atlanta was the city to live in. It was thriving with opportunities for people of color, the cost of living was comparatively low, and Stone Mountain just happened to be a place where you could buy a super-large home with a massive yard for a modest price.

"But it's Klan country," she rebutted.

"I don't care," I shot back. "Are you kidding me? This is America! How dare anyone think they have the power to monopolize opportunity in this country anywhere—and I mean anywhere? This is now my country, and nobody will dictate where I can live, what I can achieve, or what I can aspire to dream."

It was my friend's turn to look at me like I was the psychotic.

"You got some nerve," she said almost resentfully.

"Yes. That's right. And you should get some too!" I said quietly.

* * *

Integrate Stone Mountain we did, not as social activists, but as relentless pursuers of The Dream, as individuals who refused to be intimidated, and as those who looked past race and refused to see race as an inevitable obstacle and barrier to progress and achievement.

I believe that when potential intimidators see blood in the water, like sharks, they circle in and feed on their prey. Fifteen thousand fearless immigrants descended on a town in a few years. My neighbors were polite. My grandmother went to her all-white church, and soon she was its most beloved parishioner. I stood at a bus stop at 5 a.m. one winter day after the massive 1985 earthquake had hit Mexico City. A white woman, poor and living in some trailer park, she said, struck up a conversation with me. She thought I was Hispanic, although I told her I was from Jamaica. She said she was devastated over those Mexicans dying in the earthquake. Did I know how she could donate at least ten dollars to the victims in Mexico? She'd lost her electricity the week before because her husband had lost his job. I remembered crying on the way to work. Thirty-two years later, I am unable to recall if I was crying for the decimated lives of the victims of that horrific earthquake or for the look of empathy and utter desolation on that poor woman's face. Perhaps I was crying for both. But, I remember clearly that this was Stone Mountain, Georgia, 1985.

* * *

During the years of unspeakable struggles that I experienced in America as I worked up to forty-five hours a week, sometimes three jobs at a time, and attended university full-time before earning a scholarship to complete my PhD in philosophy, I bonded with other Dreamers. They were legal immigrants and aspirants whose emergent identities were forged in the crucibles of their adopted country. Like me, they worked hard and graduated *magna cum laude* from their universities—every single one of them. I should tell you about some of those Dreamers—as if they are not already part of the American folklore and actual moral mandate that continues to lure countless Dreamers to America.

There was Thai, a young Vietnamese man with whom I worked while stuffing envelopes in a bank to pay my way through college. He wasn't qualified to do much else because he could not speak English. But, he would visit me on campus at Georgia State University.

There was Vanessa, a tall, deeply black-skinned woman from Trinidad who had actually fled Trinidad because she was too dark-skinned to feel welcomed there.

Rema was a young woman from Iran who had narrowly escaped that country when her family found out she was a lesbian and used the love in their hearts for her to send her to America for her own protection.

Dinesh was a very dark-skinned, nineteen-year-old from India who was regarded as a Dalit, or "untouchable," in his country, and whom everyone in our circle of friends—Southern white, black, and foreigners from all over the world—embraced as an equal because he had the whitest teeth anyone had ever seen, we joked. But, really, it was because he had the sweetest, forgiving, and most benevolent disposition toward life that any of us had ever experienced. He was aiming for a degree in finance and then architecture.

Then there was Isabella from Guatemala whose mother had worked as a maid. Her accent was hard, working class; she was watching a lot of American television, she said, to Americanize it. Her mother had dreamed that she'd become a teacher and come back to their country and give back to the community. She wanted none of that. She wanted to become an anesthesiologist. The more often she put people to sleep, the more they'd shut the hell up and not judge the way she spoke, she once told me in the library. She'd said it quietly and then laughed and said she was only kidding. Medicine had always fascinated her.

Anyway, we all adopted Thai. We drilled him in English. Killed him with it. Even Isabella did. This was around

1989. We told him to watch a lot of television. I plied him with books and spoke to him every day in my very formal English. We all talked to him as if he were fluent in the language—every day. We took no pity on him when he looked confused. We asked him for his opinion on President Reagan, on the upcoming elections, on the Madonna video with burning crosses and depictions of her kissing a black Jesus. He had not seen the video. "Go watch it," we all said in unison. Start auditing classes, I told him. What? Yes. Just sit in on classes, sit in on my philosophy classes. This is America, I said. I'll tell the professors you're learning English and that you can't get into college because you haven't yet mastered the language. They'll be happy to have you, I assured him. *They'll feel good about themselves*, I thought. This is America, home of human benevolence and simple kindness.

Some of the detractors of America write that The Dream is the enemy of all of us, that it thrives on generalizations, on limiting the number of possible questions, on privileging immediate answers. The Dream is the enemy of all art, courageous thinking, and honest writing.

The pursuit of this Dream saddens some of America's detractors, one of them being Ta-Nehisi Coates, one of the leading black American writers, who writes that all people who pursue The Dream are lost "in a specious hope." The

Dream, he believes, was built on "the progress of those Americans who believe that they are white," and that progress was built on looting and violence. This is the record of American history, he writes in his book *Between the World and Me.* "White America" is a syndicate arrayed to protect its exclusive power to dominate and control our bodies.... However it appears, the power of domination and exclusion is central to the belief in being white, and without it, "'white people' would cease to exist for want of reasons."

I am left saddened by a deep concern that white people in general seem to wield a great deal of metaphysical power over the exercise of Coates's agency. And, it is done to such an extent that in making an enemy of The Dream that is a constitutive feature of American identity, he has irrevocably alienated himself from the redemptive hope, the cosmopolitan inclusive unity, and the faith and charity that are necessary virtues for a nation such as America. A nation, I mean, that exists in a process of moral becoming to move ever so closer towards achieving moral excellence. But, most of all, it is the unyielding and unbreakable confidence in the self that The Dream coauthors and inspires that I'm afraid he has condemned in the name of the best and noblest that exists within the most ordinary of all Americans, and all aspiring Americans.

You see, a year later, when Thai hesitantly walked alone and without support into the admissions office at Georgia State University, I told him this was America, and that he would never make it until and unless he had the confidence to assert his indubitable, *sui generis* humanity and individuality and asserted his rightful place in the pantheon of Dreamers, aspirants, and achievers. In that moment, many of us knew without resentment and rancor that he'd pass us all by. We knew, and we were proud, when, a year later, he decided that college was meant to give him the language skills he needed to open his own restaurant. Don't ask me how he did it by stuffing envelopes. But Thai, at five feet two, had saved a lot of money and, in his halting English, had convinced a bank to grant him a loan to open his own small Vietnamese restaurant. Alone. With no help from family—they were all back in Vietnam, illiterate peasants too poor even to visit, let alone assist financially. We celebrated the American way, poor as we all were, by buying him gifts, a beer, and a dictionary, because, in America, envy of achievement is not *de rigueur*. Inspiration and tearful pride were what we felt. I later learned that twenty years later, Thai did, indeed, earn his baccalaureate, *magna cum laude*, not because he had to, but because he could and wanted to. That's the American way.

In the thirty-two years I have lived in this great country, I have never once actively fought racism. As I have said, I have simply adduced myself as evidence of its utter falsity and moved forward with absolute metaphysical confidence in the world, knowing that the naming power of people who are white does not have any power over my self-esteem, my mind, my judgments, and, above all, my capacity to liberate myself through my own efforts.

Coates's book is an elegant and poetic elegy written to his son on the question of how one should live within a black body inside a country lost in the American Dream. And, here lies an injustice he has done to his black son. He writes: "The fact of history is that black people have not—probably no people ever have—liberated themselves strictly by their own efforts. In every great change in the lives of African Americans, we see the hands of events that were beyond our individual control, events that were not unalloyed goods."

I do not believe Coates intended to mislead his son; however, in imparting this philosophical credo, he may have potentially paralyzed his son for life unless the latter reappraises his philosophy and rejects it. Coates has concomitantly communicated precisely why many blacks in this country have been alienated from their own creative individual agency and emancipatory capabilities.

The most beleaguered people on the planet, the Jewish people, who have, unlike any other people, faced prosecution and persecution from their birth and continued to do so until the creation of the State of Israel, and who have lived as a diasporic people, are the biggest refutation of Coates's claim. Whether they labored in slavery in Egypt, clamored in Palestine, made magnificent contributions to human civilization in European capitals throughout the centuries, or sojourned in Africa and Asia, no one gave these heroic people an affirmative action visa to work anywhere. In spite of vitriol and invidious comparisons to vermin and pigs, despite being subjected to countless pogroms and mandated ghettos, they thrived and flourished because not even for one moment did they ever believe that their struggle for liberation lay in hands other than their own.

Coates and so many other blacks who labor under a diet of abject victimology have alienated their children from their birthright through a steady dose of repudiation and renunciation, and they have afflicted them with a sense of their own moral inefficacy and impotence. They have squashed their heroic chance of being an engine of change in the course of history. Coates tells his son: "The entire narrative of this country argues against the truth of who you are." But, this is the United States of America— born with a terrible birth defect, which was slavery; still, it is a work in progress. A country that says once more to me, to Vanessa (a woman too black to feel at home in her own country, which is predominantly black), to Thai, to Dinesh (whom no one would dare touch in his homeland): *I am an open canvas, enact and write your script on me. Without you and your story and your narrative, the story of America is incomplete*. This is the America where you can suffuse its vast landscape with an original assemblage of who you are and partake in a dialogue of who and what the nation is and ought to become. Coates tells his son that by constitutional design, his voice does not, cannot, and will never matter. Coates has banished him to a lifetime of alienation from his birthplace and, *a fortiori*, emblazoned upon his soul the moral vices of passivity and resignation. Let us hope his son rejects them.

Of the American people, including his own friends, the Dreamers, Coates writes: "They were bound because they suffered under the weight of The Dream, and they were bound by all the beautiful things, all the language and mannerisms, all the food and music, all the literature and philosophy, all the common language that they fashioned like diamonds under the weight of The Dream." This is, he says, "The Dream of acting white, of talking white, of being white.... Do not accept the lie. Do not drink from the poison." This dream, he says, is The Dream that draws lines around the ghettos and murders. He writes: "The killing fields of Chicago, of Baltimore, of Detroit, were created by the policy of the Dreamers, but their weight, their shame, rests solely upon those who are dying in them." He warns his son to be wary of The Dream, of every Dream, and every nation—especially his own. The Dreamers, he writes, "will have to struggle for themselves, to understand that the field for their Dream, the state where they have painted themselves white, is the deathbed of us all. The Dream is the same habit that endangers the planet, the same habit that sees our bodies stowed away in prisons and ghettos."

The image of a man in the world that he has communicated to his son is that of an aborted embryo, red froth dripping from its mouth, useless stumps in place of where powerful arms commanding a universe should be, screaming in abysmal terror and hopelessness at a world that he describes as both terrible and beautiful, but which he cannot change, and that he is the legatee of a personal destiny over which he has no control.

"The birth of a better world is not ultimately up to you, though I know, each day, there are grown men and women who tell you otherwise," Coates writes. If the birth of a better world is not up to him, then on whose shoulders does the responsibility fall? Does he not have an obligation to himself to suffuse the world with values and virtues of his own making? Does he not have an ethical responsibility to create, in his own moral character, the world he desires to see exist before him? Whom does he expect to manufacture a better world for his son?

You see, this man, in his deepest being, regards himself as nothing more than an assemblage of crass materialism—nothing more than his body, so his own moral imagination has become stymied and morally compromised to the point where he has relinquished his personal responsibility to make the world a better place. Why pass that passive resignation and denouncement of the world on to his son?

Perhaps, it seems, he's found the answer. "The problem with the police," Coates writes, "is not that they are fascist pigs, but that our country is ruled by majoritarian pigs." I take the term "ruled" to be a euphemism for populated by pigs. And, so, to challenge the police is to challenge the American people who send them into the ghettos armed with the same self-generated fears that compelled the people who think they are white to flee to the cities and into The Dream. There. He's said it. He's indicted the majority of the American people on some serious charges, and many of them (not all) in their curdling guilt and solvent shame will pacify him and condescendingly grant him and his indiscretions—as only the truly privileged can—a moral pass. Some will feign outrage, but most, like aristocrats who have

reversed roles with the plebeians at the European Diony-
sian bacchanals, will assume a mask of contrition, appeal
to some imaginary redemptive moment in the higher regis-
ters of their innocent conscience, and simply move on. His
accusations will make interesting dinner talk among the
cognoscenti and literati in New York City's Upper West
Side and other chic liberal bourgeois enclaves, where some
believe moral masochism and symbolic self-flagellation
are signs of virtue. Most white people, even those who
are his patrons, will feel mild contempt for him, for they
know Coates fetishizes history and is trapped in it. This
man wakes up every morning and thinks his black body
is trapped in Mississippi circa 1950. This man, perhaps
more than any other black writer in America, is dread-
fully scared of white people. And, the price he makes them
pay is guilt. Relishing in their feelings of superiority, that
in the 21st century they can make a black man feel such
fear even of progressive whites, they stoke his fears through
their support of his literary work. The more he wails and
rails against the metaphysical power of whiteness, the more
smug and entrenched they are in their own sense of racial
superiority—and the more incentive they have for him to
work his lugubrious and overly sentimental cant on their
ironically detached sensibilities.

His son, however, and countless other young black men, will be left with the impression that they lie outside the historical process, that they are not free men, and that, in being outside the realm of history, their metaphysical impotence makes all talk of pride in ancestry and peoplehood and the beauty of the black body nothing but worthless rhetorical bromides and incantations on an outdated theme of Negritude. Coates's appeal to some special black racial essentialism is affecting and sympathetic. He writes: "My working theory then held all black people as kings in exile, a nation of original men severed from our original names and our majestic Nubian culture. Surely, this was the message I took from gazing out in the [Howard] Yard. Had any people, anywhere, ever been as sprawling and beautiful as us?"

Unfortunately, there is nothing special about the black body. There is nothing special about any physical, racialized body *per se*. Black skin does not convey nobility. Neither does white skin or yellow skin. Your body is not special until it conjoins itself to a mind and adapts nature to its needs and desires and rational aspirations, its self-actualization and manifested agency. Any human body that fails to achieve a self-cultivated moral character and inscrutable human will is merely an ecological social ballast: ignoble, exploitable, and a heap of unintelligible junk on this earth.

This abnegation of absolute and total personal responsibility assumes its logical end in Coates's utter failure to grant black people responsibility for their own lives in the phenomenon of black-on-black crime. He tells his son, "Black-on-black crime is jargon, violence to language.... To yell black-on-black crime is to shoot a man and then shame him for bleeding." Why? It's a pathology that has to be reckoned with. He gives no reasons. Later, I shall contend with one of the real existential threats to blacks flourishing, which is not white people, but certain pathological traits and features within the black communities. Black-on-black crime, as I will explain, is the result of the most pernicious form of racial profiling among blacks. When blacks racially profile other blacks and kill them at a disproportionate rate than whites kill blacks, the media is silent, and the pathology is causally linked to the residual effects of slavery and the legacy of Jim Crow.

Coates's derogation of black agency is appalling. The police officer who killed Coates's friend Prince Jones was black. Prince Jones was shot and killed by a police officer who claimed that Coates's late friend had tried to run him over with his Jeep. Coates writes of a schoolyard bully who first apprised him of his place in the world by revealing a gun at his waist. In brandishing the weapon, he writes: "He let it be easily known how easily I could be selected." He was a black kid. He writes eerily of the black kid's haunting presence in his life. Throughout his letter to his son, black people are mostly treated as mindless automatons who can't seem to help themselves—and he applies this idea of help-lessness to violence. He quotes his own father who justified beating Coates by announcing, "Either I can beat him, or the police." That's all there is to it?

In his world, black-on-black crime is mono-causally reducible to the machinations and maneuverings of the Dreamers who orchestrate a system that also, so it seems, rules the neurons and synapses of the black brain. Has Coates told his son that he is twice as likely to be murdered by another black man than by a white police officer? Perhaps not, because it would not make any difference. The gang members and black individuals who kill others, including blacks, are certified moral icons who deserve dispensation because, in his reasoning, they are powerless before the street crime of history that brought the ghettos into existence.

In Search of the Moral Meaning of America and the Metaphysical Insignificance of Race

Ta-Nehisi Coates, like many on the radical far left— or the alt-left, as they should be referred to, including Cornel West, bell hooks (Gloria Jean Watkins), Michelle Alexander, and the American traitor and former Weather Underground domestic terrorist, Bill Ayer—get race in America wrong because they get the fundamental moral meaning of America wrong. To understand the real dynamics of race and its interface between the individual and society requires understanding the fundamental moral meaning of America. I discovered the moral meaning of America early on in my perception of American society. In fact, it was during the end of my undergraduate years that I truly began to fathom this meaning. I cannot communicate to you the anti-American sentiment, the actual hatred of America that is a constitutive feature of the academic left in this country, especially found in the humanities and social sciences. There, I found a phalanx of bourgeois Marxist professors extolling the virtues of communism and social-ism but living off the profits of a capitalist system. I and another immigrant friend of mine, an African woman from Cameroon named Ozong, referred to them as "welfare scholars." They had nothing good to say about America. For them, the United States was an imperialist swamp that had gutted the nations of the world of their autonomy and dignity. I and other immigrants had witnessed America using taxpayers' American dollars to uphold faltering foreign economies that were eternally regressing (including our own), offering innumerable amounts of humanitarian aid to chronic natural disaster-stricken countries, wiping whole countries free of their debts, and altruistically giving grants to countries that openly professed hatred for the very hand that was mitigating their suffering. But, the professo-riat and the radical left saw a rapacious and diabolic force at work: a maniacal will-to-power on the part of America to impose its way of life on other nations and peoples.

As I finished my electives in sociology, post-modernism in French literature, audited a class or two in black studies (just to see what was up there), read all I could in the field of women's studies, and read, in my spare time, myriad articles in continental philosophy and post-colonial studies about the evils of late capitalism and its destruction of the black and working-class family in America, I often felt as if I were living on some decaying planet.

The world I was perceiving around me, the world of my immigrant family friends from Jamaica and other Caribbean islands, and those whom I had met from Africa, Central America, and Asia who had come here with little money, and who had procured loans to start their small businesses, did not correspond to the stories about the evils and destructive nature of capitalism. I thought about a distant friend of my mom's who had brought her five children to America from Jamaica. Her name was Margaret. She had very little formal education; however, she had cultivated a talent for floral arrangements. She got a job at minimum wage, I'm guessing, in 1987 arranging flowers at a local florist in a mostly all-white neighborhood. I'm not sure what happened, or how it happened. In typical Jamaican style, of course, she worked up to two or more jobs, but, by the end of two years, she had her own thriving floral store. I believe the irony of it all was that she eventually ended up hiring one of her former supervisors at the old store to work for her! The moral of the story is that the so-called evil capitalist system had made her a thriving independent entrepreneur who would never be (and had never been, in fact) a parasitic dependent on the welfare state. She eventually put the youngest of her two children through college, bought a lovely house, and opened a second floral store.

More tellingly, I thought about Mike, the semi-literate, very black-skinned man who mowed my mother's lawn at her Atlanta home. Like several very poor Jamaicans, Mike could barely speak standard English. He started out with a cheap lawn mower and mowed my mother's lawn every two weeks for a tawdry fee. Over time, he must have earned the admiration of a neighbor as he was asked to service the neighbor's lawn, as well. In a few months' time, Mike was servicing the lawns of seven neighbors. After a year, Mike purchased a tractor mower and was—not surprisingly— serving the entire neighborhood. After two years, Mike acquired his own landscaping service with four tractor mowers and had three Mexican immigrants working for him. He was quickly able to buy his own house—twice the cost of my mother's, I believe—and bring the rest of his family to the United States.

I once asked Mike how the white people were treating him in the neighborhood.

"They pay me on time," he replied. "Sometimes before I cut their lawns."

Mike was thrilled and shocked by this arrangement, which contrasted sharply with the payment system that existed in his homeland, where he was paid next to nothing and was often in a protracted struggle to be compensated on time. Often, his own employers weren't paid on time, so how were they expected to pay him on time? To him, white people paying him promptly was a show of deep respect, a sign that they took him and his services seriously. Several of his clients would bring him a tall glass of water—"In *a real glass*," he would say in wide-eyed astonishment. This was in sharp contrast to the way he was treated in Jamaica, where he'd probably have had to quench his thirst by squatting over a garden hose and drinking from it.

"They treat me nicely," he said with a smile on his face.

The point for Mike about his relations with his white clients was that, in his existence with them as an entrepreneur, they treated both the social and economic dimensions of his existence in the limited context of their mutual dealings with him with care and respect. They didn't overreach in their social dealings with him, and he expected no such gestures from them. Truth be told, given Mike's quiet dignity and pride, he might have sensed patronization in this sort of solicitous behavior. The requisite degree of warmth that ought to mark all professional exchange was clear and present. And, that was sufficient. Far too often, left-wingers expect that whites in their dealings with blacks need to elevate the social dimensions of their associations almost to the level of some deep social intimacy that smacks of inauthenticity on all sides. But, if that is the case, then, conversely, blacks also need to see whites as just in need of social elevation in their eyes to level the ontological playing field. But, such is not the case in the liberal imaginary, and therein lies the betrayal of the insidious racism of the liberal mindset. Black social inferiority is the assumptive standpoint in need of elevation, while white innate metaphysical elevation is the normative standpoint.

I believe one of the reasons that we as immigrants have overcome is that we reject the untenable basis of this malarkey. We need no social uplift from any social or racial group. Actually, the concept of social parity is a strange notion to immigrants. We want to achieve the goals that we set for ourselves. I have never met an immigrant for whom a goal included being the social equal of any one, period, or joining the country club of an all-white group. The goal itself is degrading and absurd!

* * *

Around this time, I was befriending a young black American separatist by the name of Tariq, who believed that America was fundamentally corrupt and inimical to the authentic expression of black agency. He was twenty-six years old, attending both Morehouse College, a historically black college for black men, and auditing a few classes at Georgia State in order, as he put it, "To see how the white man's real indoctrination process was at work." Tariq was convinced that I and the other immigrants who were making it, or who were convinced we were making it, would ultimately fail because the white man would eventually take everything we had achieved right out of our mouths. I jokingly reminded him that the Second Amendment was alive and well and, as a defender of it, I'd get a gun and defend my possessions and achievements.

Tariq was an endearing fellow. Soft-spoken and gentle by nature, he was a firebrand, nevertheless, in his convictions. He constantly bought me Afrocentric books, all of which I read with great care and discussed with him respectfully. He couldn't decide if he should be speaking Ebonics since English was the language of the oppressor, and had been thrust down his throat and the throats of others. When I told him Ebonics was non-standardized English, and that when he spoke it, he sounded like he was trying to communicate in a broken second language, he grew angry. At the very least, you need to be bilingual, I told him. He agonized over Western dress forms but felt like he'd be an impostor if he started donning African garb, especially since none of the Africans on campus wore traditional African clothing. He professed not to hate white people. He just didn't want to be around them, so he was trying to create a community of like-minded people. Where? He didn't know. How? He had no idea. When? Sometime in a distant future when the right philosophy had taken root. He agonized over the fact that my degree in philosophy was in the Western tradition, and that the doctorate I had won a scholarship to pursue had nothing to do with an African philosophic system. Tariq could easily have been a precursor to Ta-Nehisi Coates, for he spoke of the American dream as a moral barometer. Those who attained it were given the moral stamp of approval. To be given this approval, he was convinced, you had to sell out and play by the white man's rules. The only moral course of action, he explained, was to act in solidarity with all those who would never achieve The Dream and reject it as a bourgeois white construct. What troubled me about Tariq's diatribes were the following: When he spoke to other black students, especially black men, it was not that they relinquished their studies and dropped out of college, it was that Tariq had the power to make them feel ashamed for planning their lives, for believing in and pursuing The Dream. He was able to drive wedges among the best within them and resurrect some shame they thought they ought to feel for their confidence, love, and optimism for America. This, I decided, was the root of defeatism, and one of the signature causes of black failure in America. It was pathological. It was not foisted on Tariq by white people. Tariq was on a full corporate scholarship financed by white people, white people who wished him well and who wanted him to succeed. But, he saw them as buying his soul for a future installment for services rendered in a society he labeled as a thriving *slavetocracy*.

I rarely debated him or tried to convince him otherwise. I thought how I and my cadre of immigrant friends and fellow mainstream black American friends who were also striving for The Dream would convince him by example or make him see reason in his errors of cognition.

"You're a slave in the white man's house," he said to me angrily one evening in the Quad. "He's colonized your mind."

I simply looked at him without moving or saying anything. And then he hissed these words when I told him that each person, ultimately, was responsible for his or her own fate:

"You are an abomination to the black race—a profligate sellout."

I thought about the sacred covenant I had made on the plane over to America a few years back. I thought about how deeply in love I was with my adopted country, and how that love kept growing, viscerally and rationally, through well-thought-out convictions about the greatness and nobility of this country. I faced Tariq squarely and said:

"And you, Tariq, have not just fallen into error. You have irrevocably passed into corruption."

With those words, I turned and walked away, and I have never spoken to him again.

Tariq had gotten the moral meaning of America wrong. It was time for me to start doing my homework and formulate a conscious understanding of that meaning and its significance to race.

* * *

Shortly before this time, I was getting much of what I can only term "racial resistance." It was coming mainly from my white, self-proclaimed progressive, left-wing professors, but whom I shall again refer to as members of the alt-left. They didn't like that I was such a rugged individualist, that I was taking intellectual pleasure in reading Ayn Rand, Ludwig von Mises, and Milton Friedman. They did not like that I had stated that I thought socialism was sheer calumny; that, as a child, I had watched it destroy my country; and that only a system of capitalism could liberate blacks and racial minorities from dependence on the welfare state. I was in the midst of applying for graduate school and was often exhausted by working up to three jobs to pay off student loans. My one-week vacation for the year from my bank job where I did sundry menial tasks was used to catch up on writing term papers—or working at Macy's as a cashier to pay bills. The problem was that I had no victim story to tell my professors. They couldn't understand my position as a conservative liberal. They found it incomprehensible, actually. But, this is the problem with the academic far left: they fail to understand how an independent black man could claim not to desire a single favor from the state. Nothing. They all told me I'd be no good as an academic philosopher because I was too opinionated. Yet, I knew that in their minds, my conservatism was compounded by the fact that I was black. The script was off. I was supposed to be a mendicant. I wasn't supposed to be as smart and articulate as I was. I needed to be more of a parasitic social dependent. But, I was struggling, for all intents and purposes, living on minimum wages, but I was free: free at last. I was independent, with a perfect credit score, paying as I went, and asking for one thing:

to be left alone! I simply wanted people not to place any obstructions in my path as I executed efforts on behalf of my sacred and irreplaceable life. I have always felt that in a free society, talented people will need very little help from others. If left free to exercise their own initiatives and luxuriate in the plethora of opportunities at their disposal, they usually make their own way.

I am sure there are several entrepreneurs among you, black, white, Asian, Hispanic, and Latino, who are still struggling, and who have not yet made it, those who have walked in my shoes and are still walking in my shoes, still trying to achieve just a patina of the American dream—waiting with your breaths held. Do not give up that part of your soul and sell it out to the haters of America who would have you believe that America and her people are constitutively racist and unjust. Your battle can be won and the greatness in your soul made to fit and accommodate any semblance of The Dream that fits the scale of your ability. Because, folks, there is no one single metric under which The Dream can be achieved, and there is no one-size-fits-all version of what The Dream looks like. The beauty of the American Dream is that its manifestation in the life of each individual is stylized by the intricate maneuverings of that individual's efforts, actions, emotions, hopes, fears, failures, and successes. It is not a formula that can be handed to you by anyone else, but a custom recipe designed and forged in the crucible of your own inviolable mind, body, and soul.

You, the single mother working as a police officer or a nurse's assistant, putting your three kids through school and paying your way, have made The Dream. You, the Hispanic or black kid who resisted the lure of the drug gangs, singled out a vision for your existence, and said *yes!* to life, are on your way to achieving The Dream. And those of you who have grown rich by your own unaided efforts deserve your fortunes and should, like the single mom or dad struggling as a fireman or a school teacher to put food on the table and who does it with dignity, should be hailed as a hero. What I have learned by living in this magnificent American civilization is that The Dream rests as much on its possibilities as it does on its outcomes, because when you look out at the world at large, you realize that the possibilities for human flourishing are a rare phenomenon, indeed. America is one of the few countries on earth that turns possibilities into forms of celebration, because, in those possibilities, we find the invaluable resources to support our visions, to extend our lives into a sunlit future, and, most importantly, to simply survive day by day when survival is, at times, the most that we can hope for in the struggle for success in life.

* * *

In thirty-two years of living in America, I have never faced the problem of radical racial resistance from white conservatives; most, if not all, simply accepted me as an individual and treated me as an equal. My race to them was neither a qualifier nor a disqualifier. It was a sociological marker that, as far as I could tell, was irrelevant to how I performed. Not one of the progressive professors during my undergraduate years encouraged me to become a philosopher. Getting letters of recommendations from them was an ordeal.

Finally, I began to understand the racism of these far-left liberals. Their sense of their own whiteness required black helplessness and inadequacy to shore up a sense of guilt, which would then prompt action on their part, from which they could seek redemption and contrition. There is unbridled hubris behind all this psychic exploitation, because one needs to posit an inferior before one can masochistically experience redemption. Redemption from some perceived wrong one has inflicted against another. That wrong, which the so-called progressive feels she or he has wielded, is white privilege. Earth hath no greater self-righteous and moralistic avenging angel than the progressive afflicted with a sense of wrongful white privilege. So, what did I do in the face of the holder of this white privilege? I committed the worst crime possible: I communicated that it was a farce. I laughed at it, made it clear I was unharmed by it, rendered the holders irrelevant, and incurred their repressed but seething wrath. Hell also hath no greater fury like a far-left-winger rejected for his or her redemptive gestures. Why?

Because if the moral meaning and purpose of your existence as a far-left liberal rests on my suffering and victimization as a black person, then you will need me to suffer indefinitely in order to continue to cull some meaning and purpose from your life. If I reject your help on the grounds that I will not let you expropriate my agency on behalf of my life, that I will cultivate the virtues in my character that are needed to emancipate my life from the hell you imagine it to be, then I've annihilated your meaning here on earth. I've identified your moral sadism in the relief of my suffering and named the moral hypocrisy of your life. It was never about me all along. It was about your redemption. You needed me to suffer so you could gain atonement, meaning and redemption. Now that I don't have to suffer (really, I never had to) you have no purpose for living. Your existence is void of moral meaning. I have, in essence, damned you to a living hell.

These alt-left individuals have a desperate need to infinitize and immortalize themselves into an indefinite future in which their relevance and need for black indebtedness and patronage never ceased to exist. They suffer from annihilation anxiety because black freedom signals the death of the very sociopolitical relevance of the far left, and not just in black lives, but in all forms of social engineering. Liberals who have staked their identity on black oppression, victimization, and suffering are moral sadists because in order to continue justifying their existence, they must continue to wish to see black people suffer under racial oppression. When this official oppression ends, as it already has, they cease being the masters of time and human destiny. They are more like conservationists or racial preservationists than anything else, and they are more like any conservative you are likely to meet, more devoted to preserving black authenticity, race consciousness, and the very notion of blackness which they love to have pitted and contrasted against themselves, since it reinforces an exotic caste system between them and the rest. Their own whiteness is brought into sharper relief the blacker and more authentically black the victims and their needs appear. Devoid of any such neediness in their own aspirational leanings, they are devoid of any stains of blackness, and, hence, enjoy a sense of racial purity. In assuming responsibility for blacks, they assume a greater share of humanity and moral agency in themselves than they do for others. They expropriate the agency of racial minorities so they can speak for them, to them, and, in essence, determine who among them is qualified to count as their racial spokesperson. Just so long as he or she plays by the racial script and respects the hierarchical ordering among the designated role of advocate and victim, all will be well. In so doing, they trespass on the autonomy of blacks and other minorities and eviscerate them of their dignity.

The sense of superiority is unmistakable. People who regard other people as their moral equals either leave them alone to make their own way, or, when they are aggrieved, address the injustice quietly and move on after it is resolved.

A far-left liberal friend of mine recently told me that she was disturbed by my views on race.

"Yes, we all need to take responsibility for who we are. But, let's face it, this message rings more hollow in some cases than in others," she declared. "Your main message that blacks need to take more responsibility for their own lives saddens me; it seems to put the emphasis in the wrong place. Is your message to women, too, that they just need to stop whining and start succeeding?"

Since I had not been aware of women besides those who were very privileged, elitist, and those entitled who were whiners, I never bothered to respond. For the most part, ordinary working women in America, possessed of a deep, independent, and pioneering spirit, are not and have never been whiners, for they know that America remains the best place in the world to be a woman. I also think that after living in several states in this great country, and after traveling to over forty countries and living in Europe for a year, it remains the best country for any gay and lesbian person, any foreigner, any religiously persecuted person, and, at this time, for a black man to thrive and flourish! Such individuals ought to know that America is not and should never be a place conducive to whiners. Whiners are anxiety-ridden individuals who have chronically convinced themselves that they live in a world in which no efficacious action is possible, where nothing makes a difference. America is and should remain tone-deaf to the pleas, cries, and lamentations of such persons. With her endless possibilities for solutions, resorting to whining is a form of renunciation and repudiation of one's country and of the creative capabilities within oneself—a stance for which few Americans will have sympathy.

I recall a letter I received from one of my readers from an article on race I had written a few months ago. He wrote:

> I am the white father of a biracial (black and white) eight-year-old daughter. I can't tell you how many people of color have told me in recent years that I have to start preparing her for the "cruel world" out there that will confront her once she is outside of my supposed protective bubble. I have read half a dozen books that deal with racial discrimination,

racial identity, etc., including Between the World and Me, *and have more on my list to read. And it has always bothered me that the message from those books and the message others have wanted me to tell my daughter is that life will be full of dangers and limitations for her, rather than that life will be full of opportunities.*

Until now, in every aspect of life, all I have witnessed for her [have] been the opportunities—even favoritism. When her school wants to market itself, it is her picture that is placed on the life-sized banner at the school entrance or in the school brochure. When we put her in theater camp, she never fails to be given a leading role in the play that results. When we walk down the street, she is routinely singled out for praise about how cute or beautiful or vivacious she is, etc. (Often to my embarrassment when other children are around us.) Obviously, appearance places a large role in all of this.

I'm not naïve enough to think that she will never face discrimination. I'm sure she already has many times, and I have missed it or dismissed it. But the concept that the world is evil to the core and what I see is some dream just waiting for the light of dawn to usher in a reality full of oppression for her has always seemed far-fetched.

* * *

There is something nefarious simmering behind the motivation of the so-called progressive sector among the left-wingers for black emancipation. As I was both struggling and succeeding in tiny steps toward success in my life, there was definitely an unmistakable and discernable attitude being directed at me.

Who was I not to be harmed or victimized by white privilege? How dare I not be a victim? How dare I deny them that power of identifying me as a victim and then emancipating me? What possessed me to have so large an efficacious agency that I could usurp and circumvent the power of this disguised form of white supremacy exercised by progressives?

Here is what I admire about conservatives. They know that one dare not possess the temerity and impertinence for finding them guilty simply for being white, and they know that any privilege they possess, whether it is brilliance, beauty, or physical prowess, is simply wasted if not exercised. If whiteness is a privilege, as is maleness, then what do people expect white people or men to do about them? Act black? Feminize themselves? Similarly, if being heterosexual is the norm (as it surely is and biologically has to be), and if it is a privilege, are straight folks supposed to start acting queer and sleep with people of the same sex? What exactly does it mean to democratize your white privilege? I remember standing in line at a car dealership years ago, waiting to get my car serviced along with a group of mostly men, black and white. The line was long, the day a hot and humid one. Along walked this blonde-haired, blue-eyed woman, tall, clad in a white see-through lamé blouse revealing mounds of cleavage, and wearing a red mini-skirt, with pavement-hurting black stilettos. She walked to the front of the line, gave her orders, and immediately had her car serviced. One of the men behind me whistled and said, "Now will you get a load of that?" Beauty had ruled the day. We chuckled and took the violation of protocol in good stride. Had she really violated our individual rights by exercising her beauty privilege?

There is an antidote (especially for those who are black) if you are traumatized by what you experience as "white privilege." Though I hate to cast any virtue in racial monikers, I would, nevertheless, say its name is: *Black Excellence*! Excellence in one's character and excellence in the cultivation of one's intellect are the best remedies for the fear of being overwhelmed by whatever magical powers one imagines that whiteness today can exercise over the lives of free people in a free society. Moral and skill perfection as goals to strive for provide one with an aspirational identity that is always in a process of perpetual development in concert with one's fellow compatriot. This striving is a process of competing with one's fellow citizens and working in harmony with and getting to know those whom one both fears and sees as one's adversaries: *white people.*

People who are forced to cohabitate and cannot be rid of each other can see themselves as incontrovertible adversaries, or, rather more luminously, as *benevolent competitors* who will inevitably have to help each other along the way even as they compete with and among themselves. The cultivation of excellence gives you a sense of not just moral and psychological confidence and the attendant sense of efficacy to perform well in the world that is its logical corollary. It also gives you a realistic assessment of those whom you have imbued with magical powers, which is what the fear of "white privilege" is all about. Your excellence becomes an operational place from which to live and thrive in the world, and because it is both a second skin in which you live, and because it forges the track record of experiences that later builds trust and confidence in your abilities, it fosters self-esteem and deep self-respect. A person of profound self-esteem who respects himself or herself is a deeply privileged human being, one equipped for success, and one endowed with traits that will shape one's destiny. Moral character is destiny.

The so-called social privilege leveraged by another person cannot inflict harm on a person who believes in the inviolate certainty of his or her moral and skill efficacy. Those who chronically complain of the unfairness of white privilege not only lack basic self-esteem, they also suffer from an appalling inability to either take an inventory of their own privileges that they are failing to cultivate or, worse, they regard the cultivation of the virtues that would indeed make them privileged as politically inexpedient since it would rob them of their victim status. There is a level of social or even metaphysical demotion in life that people are willing to luxuriate in if it permits them the luxury of elevating a perception (white privilege) to the level of a metaphysical absolute that shapes their destiny, and, ultimately, determines their fate. But, a deep commitment to a life of lived excellence is not an inoculation against anyone's privileged existence. Dignified lives are not in competition with one another. They each have their own unassailable integrity and indubitable individuality.

Excellence is an antidote to mediocrity. Excellence itself gives one a privileged life because it prepares one for every opportunity life might present. Excellence has already followed the command to rise. In the ever-continuing rise to life's challenges, using one's existence not as some site of resistance or rebellion, but as a creative solution to any challenge, causes one to see the alleged threatening "other" not as a privilege-bearing life detractor, but simply as one possessing an identity one has overdetermined. One has granted such a person too much psychological power over one's life.

I have never complained about white privilege. I have never taken it seriously as having any real causal pull in my life, nor do I trust those white people who prate endlessly about white privilege to black folks or guilt trip among themselves about its so-called deleterious effects on black lives. The reason I have never feared it—and why I can face my white brothers and sisters as equals, with love and respect and without rancor—is because I have never thought white people had any volitional power to control the manner in which I shaped my moral character, nor have they influenced my intellectual skill set in any shape or form. Seeing myself as a volitional being possessed of free will, and knowing that God has imbued no white person with a greater share of humanity than He has in me, I simply perceive reality clearly and correctly: whatever is codified socially as white privilege is and has always been weakened by the force of my personal will, my values, the unquestionable set of excellences I have developed in several areas of my life, and the habituated virtues of my soul. These have always added up—even when I was a poor and struggling student—to a very privileged existence and rarefied life.

The point is that the state cannot do anything about "white privilege," and asking white people to "democratize," "undermine," or to "socially slum down" in the name of some egalitarian principle is silly and untenable, and it is demeaning to the agency of those who make such requests.

Yet, this is not to deny that those who elongate the white privilege argument cannot cause some degree of pain in the lives of those over whom they exercise power. Years ago, after I became a full professor and the author of several books, an insidious form of racism was leveled against me. My intelligence will never be accompanied by an appeal to white sympathy or victimology, and this incurred the resentment of left-wingers who felt both intimidation and resentment. Intimidation because they were forced to accept me as a true equal. They could not *just* see me as a race writer. I was a little too white for their comfort—in their estimation.

In my firsthand experiences, I do not think most conservatives trade in that type of racial politics. Often, conservatives will say: *I don't see race.* I think this is because, historically, conservatives have been committed to a philosophy of individualism where individuals and not groups are units of moral concern. The comment used to annoy me when I was younger because I thought it was disingenuous; after all, race is a social reality. However, I'd rather be cleared of a social artifice that bears no resemblance to my deepest self-image and personal identity than be overdetermined by a social construct where all a self-proclaimed progressive is seeing is race, and who cannot bear to see me *not* see myself as a racialized person in fundamental terms. Who is more committed to a vision of herself or himself as possessing whiteness in the deepest metaphysical sense: the conservative individualist, or the progressive collectivist who must typecast the world into a set of racial players involving victims and saviors?

This is why writers such as Ta-Nehisi Coates, Cornel West, and even the nation's beloved Toni Morrison—whom I regard as an overwrought moralist who, without black angst and Holocaust-like suffering at the forefront of her literary imagination, would simply fade into irrelevancy— are lauded by the elitist left in this country. They posit a cast of black sufferers who eternally remind a certain type of white reader of the centrality of the unending potency of his or her white agency and the never-ending destructive power it wields over black victims. If West, Coates, and Morrison all stopped writing tomorrow, far-left white liberals would cease feeling white and would have a serious nervous racial meltdown. There would be no racial "others" in the room to make them aware of themselves as guilty white people who also see themselves as complicit in a world of egregious social maladies—maladies that only they as social engineering gods can fix. If Coates and his ilk stopped spitting in their faces, their sense of self-aggrandizement would disappear immediately. This is why they have issues with folks such as myself. We deny them their political, systemic, structural, institutional, and personal potency in our lives. Where such potency exists, through stealth, the cultivation of talent, strategy, and smarts, we outmaneuver them. My sense is that conservative-minded people respect this as the machinations of a self-reliant and independent person, rather than the chip-on-the-shoulder, ever-complaining resuscitator of historical grievances.

I do not fetishize history, nor am I a historical determinist. I live and write as a 21st-century intellectual—not as some cowering black man who wakes up every morning and still believes the whole of America is Mississippi circa 1950.

There is a certain type of hypocritical far-left liberal who has no black friends, claims to be a champion of racial justice, who is incensed by slights made against blacks, gays, and other minorities, and even gives their children Coates's book to read (an egregious form of psychological child abuse for which child services should be summoned, in my view), or assigns it to their students. The moral hypocrisy of this person lies in the fact that they simply want to be able to achieve some degree of articulacy in explaining black suffering to their children or their students. In explaining this suffering, they are shoring up the power they wield in a deranged society of which they are its moral architects. The cruel hypocrisy, however, is that they believe it is sufficient simply to articulate and give a platform to the voice of the sufferer. I cannot tell you how many people have confessed to me that they cannot get through a boring Toni Morrison book, with its long-suffering, angst-ridden characters, that Coates's books are so bleak and depressing, they could not finish them, or that Cornel West has morphed from an elegant and nuanced scholar into a boorish buffoon. They could take black suffering seriously—if one cares about such suffering—and do something about it, such as advocate genuine solutions and create political conditions that have been proven to ameliorate black suffering. These solutions can be a commitment to the capitalist free market system, job creation milieux, advocating lower taxes on smaller businesses, facilitating job training and mentorships programs between inner-city youths and corporations, or actually befriending black kids and volunteering time and money the way several volunteer advocates in the conservative movements do. Instead, these left-wingers espouse a verbal stream of abstract social analyses meant to make them seem like they are on the right side of history through their verbal commitments without changing history by bringing those outside the historical process—many black people—within the civilizing forces of history itself.

The second form of hypocrisy involved is one of hatred by ostensive oppression. If black victimologists hate America by virtue of their suffering and historical exclusions from mainstream society, then left-wingers can gain street credibility by enlisting their black brothers- and sisters-in-hatred in solidarity. What the bourgeois alt-left lack in personal oppression, they make up for in their righteous indignation over the plight of black victimization. And, since black victims often lack the institutional resources to showcase their suffering and perceived hopelessness to a large audience, what better way for left-wingers to make themselves useful than by atoning for their social insignificance and irrelevance by creating a performance on behalf of the victims? As I watch and hear of colleagues in the academy time and time again reporting that they are teaching Coates or this and that black writer, I slowly begin to realize it has little to do with the writers. It is all about those who take themselves to be radicals. It's all one big narcissistic show. My friend who gave his daughter Coates to read had never read him, and he found his defeatism unpalatable. Why foist that upon one's seventeen-year-old child? For the same reason the old, hip, fake, unconscionable, lip-service-paying bourgeois literati racist party hosts in the 1920s used to host their all-white parties but invited the chic, talented Negro who played the piano well: He was a spectacle for all to see, and proof that the liberal hosts were cool hipsters who loved black people and, therefore, all of humanity. After cursing them out for being majoritarian pigs and complicit racists, what could most white liberals say in the presence of a Ta-Nehisi Coates except to grin like a set of obsequious Babbitts? And, while fighting back nervous bad breath between clenched teeth grin and add: "Your book was wonderful. Just wonderful...so moved by it." Some will want to say, knowing he hates them as much as he hates those who voted for Donald Trump: "We didn't mean it. I'm not like those people you describe in your book." But, they can't say any of this. Having bought into his racial politics, they know they can't, and they know why. By virtue of their racial ascriptive identities, they are all guilty by association. God help them if they belong to the bourgeois class or the one above it!

* * *

Graduate school at Purdue University was a time for deep reading and philosophical reflection. I had taken two years off after undergraduate studies to read in every possible field—from sociology, military history, Indian philosophy, U.S. history, anthropology, the Victorian novel, the entire history of psychology, Greek mythology, and more European philosophy. Before I entered another institution of higher learning and faced a barrage of anti-American haters, it was time to prove to myself that I entered armed not with second- and third-rate conceptions of what America was at its core, but with a deeper understanding of the moral meaning of the United States. I had been in America for eight years. I was twenty-eight years old. I had strong convictions about America that I was formulating on my own over time. Burgeoning ideas that were not coming from books, per se, but from my own observations of the nature of the society in which I lived, my deep analyses of its fundamental structure, and conclusions I was drawing from reading details about the Founding Fathers and what I took to be the essential nature of America. A few weeks before classes began at Purdue, I began to consciously formalize and systematize my thinking about race and the moral meaning of America. A friend and I had formed a philosophic group called Think Twice, in which members discussed sundry political topics from a philosophical perspective. I decided I'd share with the group what I thought the moral meaning of America was and why I thought the concept of race was a betrayal of Americanism. Let me now share with you some of what I articulated to that group.

* * *

Race, I declared, had been endemic to American life from its inception. But, race, I contended, was always metaphysically (that is, in the objective nature of reality) irrelevant to the true spirit of America. Race, like slavery, was a betrayal of the essential moral meaning of America. What I came to realize was that when people came to America, past and present, they could not adhere to their tribal lineage and ancestral past in any substantive way as a means of granting them a moral identity. Immigrants who arrive in America, while cosmetically hanging onto their tribal lineage, do not in any fundamental sense appeal to tradition and custom and the old countries as ways of authenticating themselves over time. One lives not by appeal to ancestry, but by acts used to ratify the validity and legitimacy of one's personal existence.

Americans are the first individualists and, by design, the first nontribal people in the world.

If the cosmopolitan has always declared, "I am a citizen of the world," which means he or she belongs everywhere in the world and can make a home in any place in the world, then the statement presupposes that there is, or that there are, such places in the world that will accept the cosmopolitan into its confines and make such a person welcome and made to feel at home. The speaker, then, if he is not to be guilty of holding a utopian fantasy, must have a real home in mind, one to which he may affix his aspirations, hopes, and physical body. Prior to that declaration, therefore, there must be such a political state willing to accept anyone who has the audacity to declare he or she is a citizen of the world.

We may say that the one state in human history that has inserted itself into the world and the global imagination and offered itself up as a home, a refuge, a place where any person can be welcomed and offered a chance to fulfill any aspiration and goal, was and remains the United States. Today, there are other countries, of course, that fulfill this goal, including Canada, France, and Great Britain. Yet, because America was founded as a nation of immigrants—a cosmopolitan melting pot—it has not only provided the cosmopolitan with an existential referent, a home, but America has also reversed a trend in political life that has marked human societies since recorded history. It has undermined the degree of tribalism at the heart of citizenship—belonging—and the notion of community by making all such distinctions not just irrelevant, but ethically untenable. The United States has transformed the moral and political prism through which we see and evaluate the status of the aspiring citizen by fundamentally changing the way we formulate the moral qualifications and credentials a person must have to become a citizen of the republic. The answer is, of course, nothing but their naked, singular humanity, with certain rational qualifiers that have nothing to do with tribal affiliation.

Inserted as a nontribal unprecedented phenomenon in the world, the United States has achieved a unique feat of *political eugenics*. Instead of being an imitator, it is a model for emulation. America has detribalized the world by offering up its model as worthy of universal emulation; it has functioned as an ethical domain in which resocialization of a certain type takes place. People are not explicitly encouraged to relinquish their tribal identities; however, they are made aware of the fact that in the public sphere, those identities carry equal weight with any other as far as the face of their public personalities are concerned, as well as their status before the law. Individuals, as such, hold their tribal identities symbolically in the United States. Their moral reasoning may be influenced by their tribal identification, loosely speaking. This prerogative is protected under their freedom to cast their moral lives in tribal affiliation and the attendant conception of the good it may yield. But, whatever the results from this form of moral reasoning, it ought not to yield consequences that contravene the rights of others. Our conception of the good, and even our choices, is constrained by a higher commitment to subordinate the impulse to impose our conception of the good on others. This higher commitment is what informs cosmopolitan justice in the United States. It is a publicly shared ethos created in an overlapping consensus among divergent conceptions of the good.

By making foreigners and strangers into Americans, the republic has made them citizens of the world by undermining and de-ratifying the spirit of seriousness grafted onto lineage and blood identity. The American by birth or, even more so, by naturalization, is the concretization of a world citizen, because what is central to belonging and citizenship are moral purpose (the inviolable freedom to create one's own conception of the good life for oneself) and a moral-political commitment to adhere to the fundamental defining principles of the republic grounded, as it were, in a philosophy of individualism. Explicit adherence to a philosophy of individualism provides the litmus test for how and when one's actions can be exercised in the world against the freedoms and rights of another. Individualism and its political corollary in the form of individual rights subordinate society to political laws derived from moral laws. This commitment to the principles defending individualism and individual rights, in a robustly political sense, my fellow Americans, gave birth to the rise of the *individual* and enacted what the honorable ancient Stoics could only have dreamed of: the creation of a republican polity that could be home to all citizens of the world by formal principle.

The revolutionary achievement of the cosmopolitan republic of America was that it reversed an erroneous idea that had influenced human thinking: the idea that the individual as a human being preceded the state. But the individual, if he is not to live as some type of disembodied abstraction, must have a state in which he can exercise his agency and, concomitantly, that state cannot be a tribal state but an open society in which belonging and citizenship are fixed by nontribal markers and determined, instead, by universal and fundamental values to which all, by virtue of being human, can pledge allegiance. The statement, "I am a citizen of the world," by the cosmopolitan, is at worst false in the absence of a hospitable and accepting world, and, at best, incomplete without any answer to the question: "Citizen in and of what type of world?" For, indeed, if the cosmopolitan is to remain loyal to his cosmopolitan values, he could not be a citizen of Saudi Arabia, Iran, North Korea, or Nazi Germany under Adolf Hitler.

Such states would invalidate his very identity as a human being and render him impotent to practice nonracial virtues. Indeed, some of those nonracial moral virtues, such as freedom of conscience and freedom of religious affiliation and association, would have been criminalized and placed him outside the realm of citizenship.

The birth of a particular political state replete with certain values and fundamental principles are what make it even possible to hold an organic and expressive American cosmopolitan identity. The American cosmopolitan needs the American state suffused with values of liberty in order to give his declaration any traction in the real world. Since human beings are relational creatures who build their identities in tandem with one another, the cosmopolitan state, though it may have tribal enclaves within it, such as neighborhoods and places of worship and personal association, remains fundamentally cosmopolitan since the loyalties to the communities do not take precedence over loyalty to the universal republic that gives it its moral and political coherence and civic identity.

America is the first country to insert itself into the world and offer itself up as a friend to humanity; it's the place where citizens from *anywhere* can belong and play a role in suffusing the nation-state with an original assemblage of who one is.

The United States is the first full-fledged cosmopolitan state for all the reasons advanced previously and more: *America encourages human beings not to search for their origins, but, rather, their destiny.* It is the first nation in human history where—in spite of lip service to hyphenated identities that are purely symbolic—human beings have been driven to flee their origins and remake themselves through a process of becoming a new specimen, often a radically new man or woman.

The cosmopolitan and nonracial moment here in America lies in the fact that in the search for destiny, a demand is placed upon each individual. In his or her inter-actions with radically different others, one is forced to revise and modify the narrative construct on which one's previous identity was predicated.

Identity makeovers are fully possible only in the United States of America. The social reality that thoroughly suffused an "Untouchable's" life in India has no existential counter-part in the United States, a country where most Americans are properly unconcerned with the term and the nefarious caste system it denotes. The "Untouchable" lands in America, she is perceived as South Asian, and, more or less, nothing more than that. Her socioeconomic mobility in America, her associations, and her right to forget where she came from are within her powers. The loss of an old identity and the attendant new one she crafts for herself is the gift that the new country confers. The role-identity to which she was born is laid to rest. She stands side by side as a doctor with a white doctor at a local hospital somewhere in Nebraska, or Boston, or New York City. Whereas, in her native India, she was stamped with the mark of closure, fixedness, and social completeness, America grants her the freedom not just to become, but to wipe her social slate clean in order to become, in order to realize her not-as-yet-self. It grants *her* sole jurisdiction over how to interpret her past and modify the narrative accretions that add up to who others have told her she was, and had to remain, for the rest of her life.

America grants her a philosophy of life that is itself a disclosure of possibilities. It is also an exposition of various actualities of being human. These actualities are the corollaries of the modes of becoming that reside in each individual, and they are the constitutive features of one's personal identity. They are the ingredients that allow one the freedom and the privilege to metaphysically earn one's personal and moral identity. Through the forging of this identity, we make our existence each and every moment that we live in America. Unlike life in tribal societies or in the old Europe, America offers no script for the enactment of a prefabricated, socially constructed identity. In the United States, each individual has to earn his life not only economically but also metaphysically in the sense that nothing is given except the protection of the right to one's own life and freedom—right or wrong—to create a life in one's own image and for one's own good. In the radical freedom that is America, each human being contains a multiplicity of destinies and is, in a socially nonrestrictive way, a compound of several other human beings she or he may meet in the streets, in the boardroom, in the hospital, at art galleries, in classrooms of grade schools or universities, at airports, or in courtrooms. In that freedom, one's biologically determinate nature, which commits one to a life of reason and rational mode of behavior, paradoxically condemns one to a wide, infinite range, and to possibilities of modes of becoming, so long as such modes are rational when realized—rational, that is, given the local context of one's life. Because human rational nature had not been properly articulated and embedded within a corresponding political milieu before the advent of the United States, man had always lived as a *phase*, so to speak, a contingent phenomenon whose almost cyclical life would repeat itself like an animal's in the absence of philosophy of and for his nature. In the Old World, he had lived by a predetermined script, one that predated his birth and that was overdetermined in that its meaning was crafted by the voices and agency of those who shaped identity and meaning long before his own personal life, choices, and actions could insert *personal* meaning into the world. It is by the insertion of *your* life into the world that the veil of obscurity is lifted from *your* life. And, it is by such means that you can construct and understand your *personal meaning*. This personal meaning has to be conjoined to a sociopolitical environment in order to detach it from your true identity as a rational being and the corresponding social identity as it is anchored in an ordered world.

What it means to be a person will involve rationally mapping out ideal possibilities that are realizable along a continuum of achievement. The living, concrete, and thriving being of America is itself both a theory of the individual who seeks to know its subjects, and a theory that shapes its subjects. It affects its subjects. America not only properly describes the true nature of the individual as an individual—it fashions it. By means of a rational political culture, America has brought you, the individual, home to yourself. All of us have become human by acts of political culture, and, in doing so, we have evolved from quasi-natural creatures into full-fledged moral creatures.

To say that man was a natural creature before the birth of the United States is not to imply that he was either uncivilized, nor a beast. "Natural" here means that man lived as a non-transcendent being, one who could never fully alter the reality of the *thing* he was born into. He was always stuck in the mode of a rigid social identity because the capacity to navigate his environmental terrain was always compromised by tradition, legacy, and reified norms, *mores*, and systems. In America, as in any free society, traditions are blasted on a daily basis. Man is free, within the bounds of reason, to reinvent himself when he so chooses. The freedom from convention is the new American way, since America was born in flight from European conventions and stultifying customs. America is about the freedom to live by the dictates of one's personal conscience in the name of an individuality that supersedes any state-promulgated edicts, propaganda, or values.

The freedom from the burden of roots and the right to forget where he came from is a cosmopolitan moment in that it places man in a deeply nontribal associative relationship with his compatriots. America gave the individual freedom to maintain his local ancestral identity in a thin manner but altered his sensibilities in relation to the future self that he or she would become and cultivate. A spiritual transformation occurs in the act of migration and settling. The distancing of oneself from roots is an act of destroying that to which the individual was born tethered.

America was the first country that incentivized the individual to prioritize the future over the past, to eschew nostalgia in favor of hope and aspiration, and, in so doing, to keep alive the pulsating energy that vitalizes a nation twenty-four hours per day, 365 days per year. Americans' symbolic attachment to their genetic origins is just that: purely symbolic, one that gives them some sense of differentiation in the compound noun that is "American." Their identity as Americans, however, supersedes any alleged allegiance they have to the country of their ethnic or national origins. Because they and/or their ancestors chose America, the meaning of the country has transcended whatever semblance of meaning that could be found in an accident. In this respect, every American born in this country, or naturalized, chooses to be an American. They do so through affirming the moral meanings of America, chief among them being the first principles on which the country was founded and the political values that proceeded from those principles, which rationally unites around the values of individualism and the inalienability of axiomatic rights that all are born with.

More than that, however, the American forgets where he came from in a very literal sense. Ties to the ancestral past are, at most, a nostalgic indulgence, with little traction in existential terms. Very few multigenerational Americans return to their ancestral or ethnic homelands. Although several pay unconscionable lip service to being Greek-Americans or Italian-Americans without having ever visited the country of their ethnic origins and are incapable of speaking the language of the country from which their ancestors came, their socialization spheres are in America and are thoroughly American with few exceptions. The foreigner-turned-American does not give the same weight to origins. The foreigner has fled from his origins, family blood, and soil. He may be haunted by his origins; however, it is elsewhere that he sets his hopes, and that is where his struggles take place. He begins the process of achieving moral maturity and autonomy by cultivating an identity separate and apart from the one he inherited from his parents and/or their immediate socialization sphere.

America creates a stirring in the soul that allows even the most ordinary of human beings to make monumental leaps over generations of traditions and customs. This stirring activates the modes of becoming that reside in each individual. But, it does more than that. It inspires the best that resides within all of us to re-create ourselves into a stylized work of moral art. We begin the arduous but exhilarating task of *morally thematizing* our lives by asking the question and then executing the answer as: *What do I want my life to add up to*?

Cosmopolitan America gives us answers to that question in the multiplicity of identity options available to us, many of them centered on friendships, family, and, more importantly, productive work. Our becoming unfolds in the drama of narratives, and our identity is defined by our fundamental evaluation of those stories. They define who we are and what we want. Narratives have a moralizing force and provide a heuristic frame, or horizon, on which identities are predicated. This horizon allows us to determine what is good or valuable, what we endorse or oppose. Rather than function as a subsumable entity under an indistinct amorphous tribal mass, the American experience makes you the unique subject of a history that is entirely and uniquely your own, replete with your own distinctive meaning. The United States is like no other, and it cannot be because it is lived from the inside (albeit relationally with others) and validated fundamentally by the imprimatur of *your* life. It is only an unparalleled individualism that marks the uniqueness and inalienability of your life that here means the inseparability of you from your own existence.

In the old tribal world, there is interchangeability among the lives of people. Indeed, the logic of tribalism is that each person is a deputized stand-in for any other because he or she bears the authentic tribal insignia that every other carries physically and psychologically. Not so in America. America allows each to be a *sui generis* sovereign in the world, while still forming a social unit within the domain of homogenous first principles, homogenous first principles that permit varied individuals the moral and political freedom to cull divergent conceptions of the good lives for themselves—heterogeneous living by means of homogenous axiomatic principles.

The paradox here is that individuals are not subordinated to society or to other human beings; rather, America strives for a balance between codified public sentiments and convention and unassailable individualism. In disputes between how a person should choose regarding prevailing public sentiments and his or her own individual orientation, the ethos of Americanism is that it allows you to choose your conscience. In this respect, we come to understand why America has never had a mob or members of society who could be termed plebeians. While not all persons are geniuses, each harbors the seeds of his or her own exceptionality by belonging to a general society in which you do not have to yield to the yoke of convention. Originality in action and thought are what have made America and its people (all of you) exceptional in fundamental terms— from its dominance in politics, entrepreneurship, science and the arts, to its ability to inspire millions around the world to want to become Americans. This does not mean that *everyone* chooses to be exceptional. At any given time, an age can collapse into one of enshrined mediocrity and conventionality where exceptionalism and eccentricity are frowned down upon, and coarseness and vulgarity are taken as norms foisted upon an unknowing public.

It does mean, however, that a culture that nurtures exceptionalism and does not routinely enshrine mediocrity is one that will inspire people to reach for the best within themselves and share it—to infuse the world with their originality. Heroism and the possibility of ongoing originality are always on the horizon. The heroic can be impeded on by the rule of mediocrity; but, as long as human creativity is granted some small space in the crumbling confines of a culture, it can still function as an incremental installment on the human ascent towards greatness. Mediocrity, like evil, is impotent because it can destroy, but it cannot create anything of value. In the vacuum that might be left as a result of decades of rule by the cult of mediocrity and the concomitant cultural bankruptcy, some gesture of even muted grandeur rises to fill the void. Such women and men who avail themselves will always halt the full decline of a culture's trajectory towards a precipitous decline because their own heroic venturesome quest for solutions will prevail. America has always been a problem-solving country. That is part of her moral meaning. America has been such a country in various ways. That is, one coarsened at times by mediocrity and convention, but one fundamentally possessed of exalted heroism and spiritual greatness. In the era of the American Civil Rights Movement, for example, as it was during the Civil War, the moral meaning of the United States was brought into sharp focus by two rival conceptions of humanity, two models for social living, and two differing testimonies to the application of political principles to the problem of human survival. In both cases, we witnessed social upheaval out of which arose the application of political solutions to solve moral conflicts. New moral vocabularies did not arise from both conflicts; rather, existing moral language was used judiciously in a particular manner to redress and rectify systemic problems that had lain morally invisible for a long time. The result of protracted struggles framed and couched in a particular moral vernacular lead to *a moral, not a political, revolution.*

This means, in concrete terms, that America itself existed as a new method of framing claims of justice by widening the scope of who could be included in discussions of justice. The moral grammar of justice had been up for grabs ever since the inception of the nation and its inheritance of a brutal and grossly immoral system of black chattel slavery. Clearly, the heteroglossia of justice claims issued against the state did not initially include slaves and women and, to a lesser degree, non-propertied white males. But, one may see, with a degree of historical accuracy, that since the creation of the United States of America, the moral grammar had and continues to be on a continuous path towards self-reflective improvement.

We are a reformed society. And, you, all of you reading this, are a reformed people. No other country has ever included within the domain of the ethical such units of moral concern during so short a time in its nascent existence as the many persons and groups have in America. Nearly two hundred and forty-two years after its creation, there are no persons or individuals who, on principle, can be excluded from the domain of the ethical and of justice.

There have been and shall continue to be concrete examples of individuals who have been excluded; however, as we are here dealing with an interpretation of fundamentals and not concrete and empirical minutiae, it is safe to say that part of the moral meaning of the United States lies in its ever-widening pantheon of inclusiveness. This country of yours—this, the first immigrant country in history predicated on civic nationalism—includes the membership principle, but transcends it in that persons beyond its shores such as immigrants, refugees, stateless peoples, and other victims of political and economic oppression are both welcomed and invited into the United States to seek more than just ameliorative and reparative status in the republic. They achieve restitution of their moral agency and the acquisition of a political personality. They enter a republic with an exit clause that does not penalize them for exiting its borders, and the restitution of their moral agency means that they can partake in a plethora of experiments in living

73

and create or discover for themselves an endless assortment of conceptions of the good life.

This is America, where a Third Founding (taking Lincoln's promise at Gettysburg and the Civil War as the second) was achieved in the Civil Rights Movement and the momentous passage of the 1964 Civil Rights Act. The inclusive promise of We the People was finally delivered to all peoples in this country. The formal debt owed to black people for centuries of enslavement and inexcusable mistreatment and exclusion from mainstream American society was paid.

America has always been a place of regeneration, renewal, and self-examination; a place where peoplehood is not a given or a smug achievement, but, rather, a long and continuous aspiration.

These are the reasons why, in fundamental terms, the true moral narrative of this country bends itself to accommodate the shape of who I am at the core. It makes me a coauthor in the narrative script of who I wish to become, and that script becomes part of the identity of the American story.

There is a reason why Matilda the maid from Africa or Mexico or Jamaica, oppressed as she might feel by a dominant class structure in her native country, can flee the hermetically sealed nature of those systems and come to America. There is a reason why boatloads of peasants from Haiti and Cuba and other countries have risked their lives in makeshift rafts and leaky boats to seek hope and a better way of life here in America. These people are largely black people. America gives all of them a space to negotiate its ongoing moral narrative, and that's the reason why the Dalit from India who has no empowering narrative in his own country can come to find an empowering one, one that he coauthors. Matilda, the despised African maid in her hometown, and Dinesh, the dirty Untouchable in India, come to America and are given a clean slate. They are made to feel clean and worthy of being *someone*. America is a washboard that gives them a metaphysical makeover; it does not penalize them for their roots and past and hold them hostage to their lineage.

America was the first country in the world to make a Dinesh possible—to reverse the accident of his birth from a tragic state of affairs and transform it into a thriving new beginning. Why? Because the new republic was a different kind of political configuration in which the traditions and baggage of customs of the old tribal ways stifled the creative possibilities of modes of becoming, and the emergent selves that lay buried under mounds of dead-weighted and lifeless non-initiating anti-life forces were not allowed to exist in the new country. America was and remains an inspiring command to the Dineshes and Matildas of the Third World to forget, in a sense, where they came from; that is, to refrain from treating their inherited social identities with the invariability of a law of nature. Those social identities were contingencies that had to be modified if one were to have the freedom and confidence to forge one's way in America and to see everyone else as one's equal.

America gives each and every one of us that chance to have a *metaphysically clean slate*—if one wants to be clean and psychically robust and healthy. No other nation allowed individuals to play this role of a god in their lives by grafting a political milieu that would permit them to transform their lives in accordance with their conscience and moral imagination. Americans don't care where you come from and who you were, in fundamental terms. They do care who you are becoming and the future horizon over which you will spread your ever-evolving identity. They do observe the ways in which you shape your destiny in accordance with the nation's receptive individualistic ethos. This is the principal feature of American individualism.

America works!

She works for all her people on the most general level because of this all-pervasive commitment to individualism and to the individual as an individual.

But, she also works because America is an assimilationist country. It encourages assimilation. A country that encourages assimilation is not one that is *fundamentally* predicated on a logic of contagion and contamination. It is not one that seeks to inoculate itself from the sensibilities of foreigners and their alleged strange ways. It is one that believes also in reciprocal assimilation; one that believes that it has much to learn from the stories, mores, and values of its new immigrants. Yes, there have been embarrassing exceptions in America's history where the Irish and the Chinese and the Mexicans and Italians and others were thought to be contaminants of a pure nation. And, America's historical treatment of blacks has been a national tragedy and colossal disgrace during various periods in the nation's moral development. But always a nation living and breathing as a work in progress, the United States has increasingly moved beyond these prejudicial tropes into a more universal and cosmopolitan moment where the despondent and dispossessed and hopeless can find hope. We must not forget that it was in America in 1903 at Ellis island that immigrants arriving to this magnificent nation were greeted by a copper statue, the Statue of Liberty, whose pedestal bears the words of Emma Lazarus: "*Give me your tired, your poor, your huddled masses yearning to breathe free, the wretched refuse of your teeming shore. Send these the homeless, tempest-tossed to me. I lift my lamp beside the golden door."*

No country that in fundamental terms believes in the inherent evil, corruptibility, and contagion of the foreigner would issue such an open invitation to peoples of the world. The spirit of the invitation was broken by the lowest within the worst of those who called themselves Americans. But, the essence of that invitation came in a clarion call for peoples of all types to be reborn into a new type of man or woman: the new American.

The word "assimilation" stems from the Latin *"simulare,"* meaning, to make *similar*—not identical. The American invitation to assimilate stemmed from a benevolent and egalitarian belief that regardless of where you came from, you could conjoin yourself by alignment to a thin commitment to political values and ideals and adapt to the customs and attitudes of the prevailing culture. A country that projects this attitude towards its immigrants is benevolent, indeed, because, at heart, it believes not only in the inherent adaptability of all peoples, but that such a quality is simply sufficient to unite all men and women into a fraternal commonwealth of unified members, each united not by blood and lineage, but allegiance to the political values and customs that give coherence and cohesiveness to the nation.

And, this is what immigrants for the most part who come here willingly offer. With an ethos of preexisting love and respect for their adopted country, they know that to assimilate is to hand over some part of their continued socialization to their new nation and compatriots. This gift-giving feature of our humanity—anathema to the spirit of every variant of tribalism, whether it takes the form of cultural nationalism or racial particularity—is the humble capacity to genuflect before the "other" in a spirit of reciprocity, in respectful brotherhood and sisterhood, and say: *I am not so complete that I can resist handing over to you some part of my continued socialization and identity formation as a human being. With you, my friend, my humanity, regardless of its origins, continues to expand and will take me to places I could never have imagined.*

It is a deeply genuflective moment in which we come as close to loving each other as strangers as is humanly possible. One says further in the genuflection: *We share a common humanity, and in the spaces of that sacred humanity, something of the Divine is achieved. I open myself as a canvas on which you may inscribe your wisdom, teachings, and generosity—or whatever seeds of it you may have discovered in your own soul.*

This country that allows you to genuflect before it and which receives the genuflection in a spirit of reciprocal openness is the first nontribal and universal nation on the face of the earth. We as Americans do not constitute a tribe. Our principles are universal ones—always have been and always will be. They seek to attract people who will contribute to the dynamism of a resplendent future, and those same people seek to enhance the God-instilled dignity and moral worth that each person possesses by virtue of being a human being. In the genuflection, we honor those who aspire to personal transformation achieved through conjoining their labor with reason, hard work, and self-reliance; we honor the venturesome and disciplined individual whose formidable will, working in tandem with those of others in the name of mutual respect for the rights and liberties of each other, can emancipate all of us from an oppressive history we might have been born into. This is because ordinary Americans have never fetishized history, nor preached historical determinism. You arrive on her shores and make of your life what you dream and imagine it can and ought to be. I believe that if you fail in that enterprise, the responsibility must lie with you. You must pick yourself up, look America in the face, acknowledge her, and move into her essence. That core is not an enclosing binding fortress, but a boundless frontier. You must walk into the frontier, quietly and calmly with your palms open, facing the universe as you did innocently at sixteen, but with the dedication of a loyal soldier, the perseverance of a martyr, and the heroic commitment of a saint to your cause. You hold the inviolability of your spirit, and the exceptionalism of your country, as a unified sacred catechism to which you pay homage as you take your life step by step and day by day. I have fallen quite a few times in my journey through the American landscape as I traverse the paths towards my goals. I have picked myself up and looked towards the frontier.

Not once has America disappointed me!

* * *

I thought again of the covenant I had made on the plane. I thought of the decision to will the first day of my real life as the plane touched down in Atlanta in 1985 at the age of twenty. I would give birth to a new self over time. America would be the gestating and protective place of nurturance to my evolving self. The thing one realizes about America after all these years is that once you stay, you are birthed *and* never fully birthed. That's the real magic of this great nation. You may retreat at any moment for renewal, self-regeneration, re-identification, re-creation, and radial reinvention. And, at the end of it all, America stands waiting for you, ready for you to reinsert yourself into The Dream until you slowly realize you never left. America leaves you free from historical determinism. In some sense, it is the most challenging country on earth because, in setting you free, it offers you no protection save the sanctity of your naked singularity. This process of reinvention and of re-identification is part of what it means to be an American, or one in the making. It is the most magnificent model of what it means to become a human being in the world we live in today because it sets no higher price to human value than the *sui generis* values of freedom and liberty.

Racial Profiling, Police Brutality, and the Moral Hypocrisy of "Black Lives Matter"

So, I'M CHATTING WITH a colleague of mine from a university in New York who is a retired college professor and who is now teaching in the prisons. We're having lunch and he's talking despairingly about hopelessness in America. I stare blankly at him and chew on my salmon salad. He asks me what I think. I tell him to be more specific. He's shocked. Don't I just see the entire hopelessness of American society all around me? Allan is sixty-eight years old, a self-committed Marxist. Both of his parents were surgeons from New York, and he attended private schools all his life. He graduated from Harvard and Princeton Universities with a plethora of degrees in philosophy and French literature. Although we're on opposite ends of the political spectrum, I still enjoy the sharpness of his mind and his compassionate spirit; but I resist, as best as I can, his dour pessimism and lugubrious sentimentality. He's got a world-weary, seen-it-all attitude. The world, according to his prognostications, is going to be felled soon by one apocalyptic, working-class, universal revolutionary blow. People are hungry in America, he says—literally! They want a change. "Socialism is the way forward," he says in a dreamy, wistful voice. He advocates an America without borders where even illegal immigrants can vote socialism into a living reality. That's the only way it will happen, he says. Empower undocumented peoples and even legal immigrants with a sense of their human rights and they'll transform America into a socialist state. People are hungry, he reasserts.

"They are hungrier in Africa and Haiti, and they are coming in droves to try to escape that form of hunger for a life in America. Maybe we should analytically distinguish between degrees of hunger," I quip.

He shakes his head.

"Jason, black men are being killed in this country."

"Oh, I know that. They are being exterminated. We both live in Chicago, where they are being massacred on a weekly and daily basis, but who is killing them? Huh?

Are white cops going in and slaughtering them? Are white people from the suburbs rifling them down? Are the military going in and killing these black men?"

"If the cops kill them, what incentive do they have to obey the law and…?"

I cut him off right there, as I know where he's going with all this. We've been here before.

"Listen," I tell him. "The spate of killings of unarmed black men by police officers in recent years is tragic and a disgrace. It is, I believe, the work of a small minority of rogue police officers, or ordinary officers weighed down by a form of statistical reasoning—given the disproportionate homicidal rates among black men—that breeds a pervasive fear among the general population of blacks, and whites of black men in general. This is sad, and it is a blight against the humanity of all persons."

I continue, "However, against the heroic commitment of the entire police force in this country, and given the enormous contribution that police officers—black, white, and Hispanic—are making every day by going into black and Hispanic communities overrun by murderous street gangs and protecting the lives of innocent residents living in these tragic neighborhoods, we need to keep things in perspective here. Police officers, when all is said and done, overworked as they are, underpaid as they are, and given the poor public image that they suffer, are doing a good job of trying to protect black lives in the deplorable and feral inner cities of this country where thugs and hooligans think neighborhoods are either extensions of their shoddy living rooms, or their own private fiefdoms to do as they please."

Allan shuffles uncomfortably in his chair and clears his throat. He wants to move the conversation to the evils of profiling. What do I think of that? I agree that racial profiling is unjust because it *arbitrarily* targets members of a law-abiding majority at any given time. Given that law enforcement agents have a coercive monopoly on the use of force against virtually helpless citizens, profiling is a legally contentious affair that, given the broad discretionary powers of the officers who exercise it, can lead to disastrous consequences. But, in the hands of those exercising discretionary powers, there was still some possibility for rationality in the exercise of racial profiling itself. That is, an officer who has made an error of judgment in singling out a person for suspicious activity based on race could revise his actions before eviscerating the person of her or his dignity. The act of profiling itself by police officers, while embarrassing and painful to an innocent person, is not irrevocably harmful. There was, however, I explained to Allan, a more deadly and insidious form of racial profiling that was taking place in our nation that was, in the name of moral hypocrisy, failing to incur the righteous indignation of all who cared for universal justice.

This form of racial profiling is done by blacks against other blacks, which manifests itself in black-on-black crimes. Here, black men in particular target other black people as homicidal victims, as prey to be annihilated. This form of racial profiling is worse than police racial profiling, and not because it is an in-group phenomenon; rather, it's because the terminal intent of its perpetrators leaves a trail of tragic irrevocable consequences. Every member and supporter of the Black Lives Matter movement should turn his or her taunting signs away from the white gaze and shove it deep into the consciousness of those inside black neighborhoods and the seeming indifference of its members who don't seem to understand that it's neither white apathy nor the average white family attending to their business and caring for their own family that causes what Allan thinks is the genocide of black people in America. The average white family has created no policies and has instituted no systemic forms of oppression that existentially force the hands of criminals on the streets.

When some black folks complain that white people don't value black lives, I often ask: *What exactly do you mean?* Too many black folks don't seem to want to hold other black people accountable to the horrific genocidal crimes they are committing against one another. The whole Black Lives Matter movement has its face turned in the wrong direction. I want to say to them: *Turn around and go back to your communities and hold up the signs there.* Why should white people esteem your lives and value your humanity when you can't condemn and express moral outrage at those who maim and kill your children in the name of gang warfare, senseless street violence, and drive-by shootings? And, by the way, why do white people have a larger moral responsibility to care about black people than black people have to care about their own lives? Why on earth are blacks in need of special white nurturance, per se?

Compared to the recent spate of police killings of unarmed black men by police, black-on-black crime is a national security disaster and risk. The moral hysteria raised by a few incidents of police brutalities in the face of this larger national tragedy is reckless hyperbole. It hides from the nation a deeper malaise at work in the psyche of some in the black community: a deep form of self-hatred that manifests itself in a homicidal rage that turns itself not fundamentally against white people, but against other black people.

Allan is uncomfortable with this form of conversation and, like Coates and others on the alt-left who belong to the "Trauma Cult," tries again to place the blame on what he calls *white privilege*. This very privilege is a coauthor of the hopelessness and despair in the black ghettos around the country. He veers non-logically into a case for reparations for blacks based on this privilege and the ways in which unfair discrimination against blacks is sociologically responsible for what I am referring to as pathologies in some of the black communities. Were the pathological disproportionate number of violent crimes committed by blacks in the United States the derivative consequence of white privilege, I wanted to know?

According to the U.S. Department of Justice, blacks accounted for 52.5 percent of all homicide offenders from 1980 to 2008, with whites accounting for 45.3 percent, and "other" accounting for 2.2 percent. The offending rate for blacks (the number of blacks who commit homicide as a percentage of the black population) was almost eight times higher than that for whites, and the victim rate six times higher. Most homicides were intraracial, with 84 percent of white victims killed by whites, and 93 percent of black victims killed by blacks. Should white society seek to foist collective guilt and shame on blacks because of the higher rate of homicides committed by black men?

By the logic of Allan's and Coates's reasoning, should black families seek reparations from the "racist state" that has systemically created the physical ghettos and economic deprivations that somehow forced these black men to disproportionately murder a number of their fellow citizens? The consistent application of that philosophy would force him into an inverted position. It would mean that any white person could legitimately look at any black person and coerce him or her into racial shame for the disproportionate murders that blacks have committed against blacks.

When people give up the seductive idea that the world owes them something, except the right to be left alone, they are given the power of forgiveness—even to those who have historically oppressed them.

This, I told Allan, reminded me of Coates's June 2014 essay in *The Atlantic* arguing for reparations for black people. He was wrong. No self-respecting black person ought to take a single penny from the state for the infliction of any ancestral damage. The very premise presupposes that blacks are wards of the state. If individual rights are currently being violated by states that illegally discriminate against blacks, that is a matter to be redressed in the courts. People who are possessed of self-esteem, who are dignified individuals capable of supporting themselves, do not seek any form of reparation. It is beneath them. Reason indicates that you cannot codify either collective guilt or collective entitlement. And, reparations are predicated on the attribution of collective guilt, which in turn is based on the worst form of racism: biological collectivism.

My lunch with Allan ended uneventfully. We had reached an impasse on the matter of the moral legitimacy of Black Lives Matter. We agreed to disagree as we usually did on most things, and, as always, we hugged and parted amicably. But, the conversational impasse had left my mind racing with more thoughts about the moral hypocrisy about a movement I had initially thought had some moral legitimacy in redressing a legal issue between the police and unarmed citizens who, in that moment of interrogation between themselves and the police, had posed no threat.

As I sat at my desk late that evening and watched the street grow dark through my window, I thought about another transgressive and unpardonable sin the Black Lives Matter movement had made and continues to make: It adopts a profoundly anti-Israel platform. It adopts a far-left, profoundly anti-America and anti-Israel manifesto that goes well beyond police brutality, and it accuses Israel of "genocide" and "apartheid." The Black Lives Matter platform that supports the "Boycott, Divestment, Sanctions," (BDS) movement, supports the view that the United States justifies and advances the global war on terror via its alliances with Israel and is complicit in the genocide taking place against the Palestinian people. Besides condemning

Israel, the Black Lives Matter platform has demanded race-based reparations, the breaking up of large banks, voting rights for illegal immigrants, fossil fuel divestment, an end to private education and charter schools, a "universal basic income," and free college for blacks.

As a staunch defender of Israel on moral grounds, I find myself categorically condemning the moral ineptitude of the Black Lives Matter movement as fraudulent, vituperative, and committing a case of the Big Lie. If there is a victim in the Middle East, it is beleaguered Israel, the only technological and democratic civilization among a plethora of illiberal, primitive, and gross human rights-abusing nations that treat women worse than cattle and don't know the meaning of religious reciprocity. Since its founding, Israel has fought invading marauders in the likes of the Jordanians, the Egyptians, and the Syrians who invaded her, threatened her right to exist, and have tried to eliminate her and Jewry from the region with the help of Hezbollah, Hamas, and the Palestinian Authority. Now, the war refugees of those countries, the people who call themselves Palestinians, have made an unprecedented demand in the history of warfare. Displaced by a war that their leaders started and lost, and claiming a right to return to a territory they failed to conqueror, they are claiming a right to return, to demand a state within a state in which they are war refugees. They are allowed by the Israeli government to become citizens, to serve in the Knesset, side by side with Israeli Jews, and to elect terrorist governments (Hamas, and the Palestinian Authority) whose charters have as their constitutive feature the annihilation of Jewry and paint Jews as pigs, vermin, and an evil phenomenon that must be eradicated.

Israel is the only altruistic country I know of that grants citizenship and land rights to its avowed enemies, who were twice offered a two-state offering to its two leaders Yassir Arafat and Mahmoud Abbas, only to be rewarded with a Second Intifada and mass murders of Israeli citizens and intransigence forged in the conviction that no deals will be made once Jews—any Jews—occupy the land of Israel. Israel unilaterally handed over its territory of Gaza to the terrorist government Hamas and was, and still is, rewarded by a daily showering of rockets from Gaza into Israel.

Black Lives Matter ought to be ashamed of itself for selling out Jews in America to whom blacks in this country are enormously indebted. If there are any unsung heroes of the Civil Rights Movement, it is the Jews in America who played an enormous but largely unacknowledged role in the liberation of blacks in America from racial oppression. American Jews played a significant role in the founding and funding of some of the most important civil rights organizations. These include the National Association for the

Advancement of Colored People (NAACP), the Southern Christian Leadership Conference (SCLC), and the Student Nonviolent Coordinating Committee (SNCC). In 1909, Henry Moscowitz joined W. E. B. Du Bois and other civil rights leaders to create the NAACP. The vice-chairman of the Union of American Hebrew Congregations (now the Union for Reform Judaism), Kivie Kaplan, served as the national president of the NAACP from 1966 to 1975. Arnie Aronson worked with A. Philip Randolph and Roy Wilkins to found the Leadership Conference. From 1910 to 1940, there were more than 2,000 primary and secondary schools and twenty black colleges (including Howard, Dillard, and Fisk Universities) established in whole or in part by contributions from Jewish philanthropist Julius Rosenwald. At the height of the so-called "Rosenwald schools," nearly 40 percent of Southern blacks were educated at one of these institutions. During the Civil Rights Movement, Jewish activists represented a disproportionate number of whites involved in the struggle for black emancipation. Jews made up half of the young people who participated in the Mississippi Freedom Summer in 1964. Leaders of the Reform Movement were arrested with Rev. Dr. Martin Luther King Jr. in St. Augustine, Florida, in 1964, after a challenge to racial segregation in public accommodations. The Civil Rights Act of 1964 and the Voting Rights Act of 1965 were drafted in the conference room of Religious Action Center (RAC) of Reform Judaism, under the aegis of the Leadership Conference, which for decades was in the RAC's building.

The hard, cold, and unsentimental fact of the matter is that without Jewish financial backing and moral contributions, there may at worst have never been a Civil Rights Movement in the United States of America, or the heroic Third Founding, which culminated in the passage of the Civil Rights Acts, would very well have been slow in its arrival. Charged with a universal duty to repair the world by God and to remedy every injustice in the world where they find it, the Jews, a peace-loving people who have maintained a three thousand-year-plus civilization without conquering any people or peoples, carried through on their promise by playing a pivotal role in widening the pantheon of the human community in America. They tweaked the moral conscience of their fellow Americans and entreated them to consider blacks and all persons of color as worthwhile units of moral concern possessed of equal dignity and moral worth just as they would anyone else.

The anti-Israeli platform that Black Lives Matter has misguidedly adopted has rightfully alienated several progressive Jews in America who had aligned themselves with the organization. In its libelous accusations against Israeli Jews protecting their ancestral homeland, the Black

Lives Matter movement suggests that in their support of Israel, such Jews are complicit in the unproven crimes of genocide and apartheid. We must remember that even in the daily onslaughts of war and terror inflicted against Israeli Jews by Palestinians, the Jews, in a spirit of almost irrational altruism, take great pains to limit civilian casualties and to ensure that those caught in a war they did not personally initiate are spared as much damage against their bodily integrity as possible.

But let us for a moment return to one of the more morally irresponsible claims made by the Black Lives Matter movement that will bring us back to issues of race that will surely offend any self-respecting fellow black American citizen. I refer to the demand that the United States provide free college education for blacks. On what grounds is this organization making such a demand? Why free college education for blacks but not for poor whites, or for Hispanic, Latino, Asian, or Native American college students? What special sociopolitical conditions exist for blacks that do not hold for other ethnic or racial groups such that blacks deserve a double affirmative action visa to enter college?

Could it be that the spokespersons for the movement are responding to another cultural pathology that blacks face: the problem of single-parent families under which 70 percent of African-American children live? Certainly, this is a social issue over which blacks have control. It is not a derivative consequence or inheritance of slavery or Jim Crow. The latter periods saw significantly lower birth rates to single-parent families. If 70 percent of black children are born into single-parent families, this is a financially untenable situation for such families. It certainly duplicates structures of poverty, but this is not a result of racism or the doing of white people. This is a failure to exercise free will in a judicious and wise manner. That free will also has a moral responsibility to be fiscally mature in managing human lives. The downward spiral of the black family, the marked absence of fathers from such homes, cannot be the responsibility of white Americans. Nor should white Americans ever be asked what they intend to do about that problem. It is not their problem. The question, properly speaking, should be posed to blacks in the form of: *And what do you intend to do about these problems and issues endemic to your communities?*

Realizing, of course, that not every single parent (usually the mother, in such cases) can afford to send her children to college, is the movement simply attempting to pass that responsibility off to society? This leads us to some significant philosophical questions. And, they are these: Are the procreative choices that we make in life the responsibility of others, or, are they our own? Do we have a constitutional right to have children we cannot afford to maintain? Is it a form of child neglect to bring more children into the world than you can afford to support? When you have children, is it fair to expect your neighbors to bear in the financial responsibility of raising them when they may have decided not to have any, or to have just one, or two, or just the exact number their budget can afford over the course of a lifetime? You who have sacrificed and planned your lives carefully and are already in debt and sending your own children to school, by what moral right would anyone dare tell you that by his or her racial identity you—regardless of your own race—have a right to finance his or her college education?

Those on the far left will say that to do so is a social good. I have heard this sort of conceptual inanity repeatedly, and I have often asked for clarification. When asked what is meant by social good, left-wingers often mean "the public interest." When asked to define the public interest, they fumble and mumble and twist themselves like linguistic pretzels into all orders of moral conundrums. Society is nothing more than the sum of each individual person. Therefore, any reference to the public good would have to first logically refer to what is the good of each individual person. The answer to this presupposes the question: How do we know what that good is? One of the glorious achievements of this country, and one that has appealed to millions the world over, is that here we get to choose a conception of the good for ourselves. For some, it is having a family, for others it is pursuing a career or devoting one's life to a specialized hobby, service to others, traveling—you name it. There are as many conceptions of the good as there are persons to imagine them for themselves. And, in the United States of America, the state has no business imposing its or any conception of the good on you or deciding *a priori* what your conception of the good is. It leaves you free to choose your own notion of the good, so long as in doing so, you do not violate the individual rights of others. Any foisted notion of the public good on individuals means that a group of people has decided that their interests and their conception of the good should be the sum of the good of all members of society. It is an act of tyranny because it overrides your conscience and takes away your indubitable capacity to decide *what* the good is for you personally.

The cardinal sin of asking for anything for free in this life is that you abnegate your responsibility not just for maintaining your existence but, more importantly, of achieving your humanity. For we achieve our humanity in several ways. One is by exchanging goods and services with others. We affirm the worth of the other, and we respect the other by rewarding him or her for such services, and, in so doing, our agency is implicated in affirming our self-worth and dignity in the beautiful act of reciprocity. In reciprocity, there is a recognition of equality among each of us as individuals. Each ratifies the survival of the other through this reciprocation.

The demand for a free education, along with race-based reparations by the movement and others in this country, is symptomatic of another problem in race relations in the United States. Those on the alt-left see self-reliance, initiative, and a commitment to one's own life as, at best, hopelessly naïve—not for themselves. Oh, no, they have gotten where they are by the exercise of their own virtues. But the state apparatus and its system are so corrupt and stacked against blacks, they believe, that the application of those virtues will always be possible for a Condoleezza Rice, or a Colin Powell, or an Oprah Winfrey, but not for the majority of blacks in America. The problem is that these left-wingers see grit, honor, hard work, and self-reliance as American virtues, and ones that they possess. But, more specifically, unlike, say, conservatives, who tend to be individualistic and encouraging of universal self-reliance, left-wingers see such traits as "white" characteristics. Those traits reinforce *whiteness* in their minds, and there is a gnawing resentment among those blacks who wish to appropriate those virtues for themselves. They cease being black in the minds of the left. A sizable number of well-meaning, but, in the end, racist progressives, need black people to be black. It's the darndest thing, but an African colleague of mine, dressed in a formal Chanel suit, was met with disappointment by her department chair at an institution I taught at nearly twenty years ago. Why, they wanted to know, didn't she wear something more ethnic like an African dress, and how come she was losing her accent?

The point I am making once more is that left-wingers heed the call of black dependence with glee because it places them in a permanent position of power, and as part of a managerial class over a needy set of entitled subjects whose interests they represent. The absence of independence, and the neediness of some blacks, simply reinforces how independent, privileged, and powerful they stand in relation to their socioeconomic inferiors.

Finally, my fellow Americans, when you demand anything for free, a demand that is so un-American one can hardly take the claim seriously, you are claiming a status of such impoverishment that you are holding yourself up as an object of *pity*. But, unlike compassion and mercy, pity is not an American emotion at all. Pity denotes contemptuous sorrow for the misery or distress of another person. And the contempt one feels is linked to a moral vice the other harbors: an unwillingness to exercise one's agency in the relief of that suffering; a perception on the part of the pitied that the world is hostile to one's initiatives, and that no action is possible—at least, action that would liberate one from the condition of hopelessness one is trapped in. We Americans find it hard to endorse that viewpoint because it assumes a malevolence about the American universe that is untenable and empirically false. No doors are closed forever to anyone in this great country of ours. If your ethos and character disposition are set for achievement, if your will is wedded to a resilient and tenacious spirit, perseverance guides and drives your efforts, and, further, you rid yourself of the squalid self-defeating idea that you are entitled to the financial earnings of other people—that your parents' procreative choices are the responsibility of other people—you will find a way to make it in this country.

* * *

I am thinking again of the sacred covenant I made with America. It is 1985. It's the drive on the way from the airport. I'd never been to Atlanta before. The greenery of the place is breathtakingly beautiful. It looks to me like a place of paradise etched, eternally, somewhere between late spring and early summer. The family friend who has picked us up wants to take the back roads to show us the beauty of the place. No, I insist. Take the highway. I want to see the *Help Wanted* signs along the way. I need to find a job by the end of the week. The look of incredulity on his face is comical.

The following day, I collect my Social Security card, and the next day, I hit the streets. I'd never taken a subway in my life. But, I'd gotten on a train heading downtown into the financial district, dressed in a suit, armed with a flimsy résumé, and applied for twenty-four different jobs that day. I applied to banks, advertising and insurance agencies, restaurants, small businesses, corporate call centers, for every job imaginable, in every capacity possible—from stuffing envelopes, opening doors, waiting tables, you name it. I thought there was dignity in decent work, and, no matter what, I was willing to do it. I was a skinny twenty-year-old kid with little muscle mass, and I was a bona fide book nerd, so I avoided construction sites! I did the round of daily job applications for three weeks until I landed a job as a credit card collector in a bank. I worked there for a year, full-time, and saved up enough money for half a year of college.

There was a maniacal drive in me. My family could not and did not contribute to my college education because they could not afford to. My mother had divorced my father when I was around seven, and, although she worked as a banker in Jamaica, she struggled tremendously to give me and my brother the best private school education in the top school in the entire Caribbean for the first eighteen years of my life. I was now a man. I entered college at nearly twenty-two—late by American standards. I was a man. My life was mine. I was free. This was my life. Inviolably sacred. It belonged to me. It was irreplaceable. I had to maintain its incalculable and nonnegotiable value. I dared not place its responsibility in anyone's hands, and certainly not in the hands of the government! Regardless of the struggle and the sometimes-menial jobs to support that life, there was no one who could take better care of it. Responsibility for it was not to be promiscuously allocated among people who, deep down inside their own souls, didn't know the value of that life.

This is what grit and commitment to decent hard work in America will teach you. Regardless of what you do, whether you scrub a toilet, practice medicine, clean someone's bedsore, or fly a plane, dignity is something you possess inside, and it is something you bring to whatever you do in your line of work. That work reaffirms your commitment to the sanctity of your life.

Your life is never cheapened by the work you do. You enhance the dignity of the work you do by imbuing it with the magnificence of your humanity, the grandeur of your soul, and the inviolability of your individuality. The work is enriched simply by your touch. That grandeur is yours. You've earned it!

* * *

What really makes us is, in one respect, way beyond knowing. At some point, we give into our lives and cultivate a script consciously or unconsciously, and we move forward, guided by that script. There is chance and there is fate, but I believe the choices we make, and the attendant actions that follow, cultivate a character that creates our destiny. I remember that the desire to come to America had always been there from as far back as I could remember. My mother once asked me during my childhood if I wanted to spend some time living in Switzerland with the Swiss side of my family. I was adamant. Absolutely not! America was going to be my destiny. How could I be so sure? I was only twelve years old, my mother said. But, America existed as an axiom in my mind. How I became transported physically, I have already told you. But, the seeds that were planted were sown in willpower and agony and deep sorrow and pain.

Jamaican Boy in Search of America

Kingston, Jamaica

IT IS 1975. I'M SITTING with my father in the sofa-like front seat of his father's car, which he has borrowed to take me for a ride. Just the two of us. It's a red car, a 1960-something Vauxhall.

I'm ten years old.

My father smells of coconut oil. He always smells good—fresh, earthy, and natural. We've just come from a long drive where he has told me to just be who I want to be.

"You were cut out to be a writer and a poet. Don't get sidetracked into thinking you have to be a lawyer or any of that nonsense," he says.

He's been on this mission to save my poetic soul. His mother has been paying for my private tutor in math and algebra, and he keeps telling me not to waste my time, that I'll never need math "because the soul of a poet transcends the exactitude of mathematics. You'll never be one of those persons trapped in arid mental categories."

In the car, we're silent. We are looking at the floor. He edges closer and puts his arm around me. The aroma of coconut oil—which he'd always used to tan his really pasty skin so now it's a rich bronze and glows a little as I look up, sadly, into his green eyes—mingles with his sweat. I can see my granddad, my mother's father, seething on the front porch. Everyone's thought of my dad as a real loser, a bum who can't hold a job. He can give his children a lot of hugs and kisses, and he sings really well to them, but, boy, he sure can't support them financially. That job's been left to my mother. Yesterday, he just dropped by and said, "Jason, ask for anything you want. Anything in the whole wide world."

"I want a lemon meringue pie."

Ten minutes later, he comes by with the biggest pie I've ever seen. I eat it right there on the spot.

We're still looking at the floor of the car, and I know that he's going to say something that will make us very sad. He's just freed me from a lifetime of school drudgery. (I don't ever have to do math, I can skip classes, and I can read grownup novels and poetry.) And now he's going to spoil it with bad news. I can sense it. The silence is unbearable.

He begins to weep. Silently. He moves in closer. His body is trembling. I see his right ankle twitching in his Jesus sandal. Beads of sweat are breaking out on his legs, and he's toying with the pleats in his denim shorts.

He says, "I love you, Jason. I love you so much. I love you more than anything and anyone else."

I feel numb and sad at the same time. I feel lonely and confused. I want to hug him back, but I just sit there, looking at my skinny brown legs. I dare to look up at his face and see something I can't write about because I don't understand it. I see a look of absolute despair. He rests his head against mine and whispers over and over again, "I love you, I love you. I love you."

I look up, wondering where my brother is. My grandfather is walking towards the car. He is shouting. He wants me back in the house, and, suddenly, my father bolts from the car and says, still crying, "I need to speak to my son. I have a right to speak to my son."

I'd never seen my father in this state. I can't recall the exchange. I only remember my grandfather's anger and the sobbing desperation in my father's voice as he defends his right to speak to his son. I eventually leave the car and my father makes one last attempt to hold me as my grandfather asserts *his* right over me.

* * *

We return to the car and sit, huddled, holding hands, weeping. Grieving right there in the open. Just the two of us.

And, I loved him. And, he loved me back.

The day before, I had wrapped my legs around his waist and kissed him all over his neck, and he told his mother, "I think my son is in love with me."

In the car, he takes my hands and tells me that one day I will go to America, that I will become a philosopher and write great books that millions of people will read. He grows sad. He says:

"The struggle, the loneliness of the early years, will take their toll on you later in life, and you will be driven to the brink of madness. But, America is your destiny and your true home, Jason. Never forget that. It is where you belong."

I ask him what philosophy is, and he smiles and kisses my forehead. He tells me I am a Warrior King and a healer whose job is to unite humanity. Then he sits back and closes his eyes and holds my hand.

He had lost his battles, had tried to take his own life twice. The world told him he was a fool, and yet he told me I was to be a writer, and that I was special.

He said he'd seen God's face and was seduced by its beauty. Some said he was possessed by the Devil because he dealt in black magic. Others said he was just crazy.

Now, it was over. This love affair with my father. Just like that. He comes to the house a few months later, dressed in a white robe, painted white boots, and a white sword tucked into a sash on his white belt. He wears a white turban over his head that stretches his green eyes into two eerie slits.

He will have to repudiate us, he says. He has been called out to do God's work, to be his servant, and to be the bride of Christ. He explains and explains. Then, what he calls the apocalyptic announcement: "Observe, my son: I am married now to Christ, whom I love more than anything else, even you."

He leaves, and he never looks back as I stand staring out into the distance, perhaps in the same spot where he'd stood a few months earlier, asserting his right to speak and weep with me.

I get this in the mail from him a few weeks later:

> *My Son, Oh my Son.*
> *How do I regret time was too short to*
> *Kiss your sweat while we played.*
> *Born prematurely old*
> *I was called out to war;*
> *Vanity was not my cause*
> *Nor the cause of my Requiem.*
> *So, although the past remains a haunting cancerous memory,*
> *It is unwise to resurrect*
> *A cold deliberate casualty*
> *Fired with the blood wrung from our twisted souls.*

I trod the king's highway towards the souls I left behind.
Solitude is my way out of madness, my son.
Loneliness is a triumphant man.

* * *

I left Jamaica ten years later, leaving behind our anguish and his despair. Truth be told, when I was three years old, he and my mother had immigrated to the States for four years, where he had tried to pursue the American Dream. He had had big dreams of being a singer. They had, reluctantly, left us behind with my grandparents in Jamaica. It should have been a four-week separation. It turned into a four-year separation. The departure and four-year separation from my parents would be the single most painful experience of my life. It broke my mother financially. It broke my father spiritually as the ravages of schizophrenia and drug addiction consumed him in New York from 1968 to 1972. My mother returned on bended knees and with open arms to her two children, heartbroken, but hopeful, I believe. My father returned a broken man who twice tried to commit suicide. In the years ahead, in his brokenness, my father tried passionately to communicate to me that it was not America that had failed him, but, rather, life that had betrayed him. He was a casualty of existence, plain and simple. Life had aborted him from the womb too early and he would have failed in whatever world reality had propelled him. My life would be different, he once said quietly. I was tailor-made for America.

* * *

My last visit to him was at his cottage in Jamaica, in the lush Blue Mountains in 2012. I can still see him kneeling in the middle of the dirt road as I drive away. His head is thrown back. He is looking up at the sky. His arms are raised to heaven, and tears are streaming down his face. And, over and over again, he is thanking God for bringing me back. "Thank you. Thank you, sweet Jesus, thank you God for delivering my firstborn back into my arms," he cries.

I am looking in the rearview mirror of the car I've borrowed. I stop and contemplate running back and throwing my arms around his neck and telling him that I love him. Wouldn't it be better to be one with him in his confused visions?

His arms are still outstretched and he looks as if he is falling into a trance. I feel as if I have entered an area where the living and the dead have exchanged places. I press the gas pedal and then accelerate, slowly at first, then quickly, and then I am gone, leaving that place forever, where reason and madness brew and come to a stalemate.

* * *

America was my escape from my father's madness, a place where I could prove that I would never be like him. America was also the land of eternal hope, which meant it was a place that kept the soul young. I believe that day in the car with my father, just the two of us sitting alone, that a burning desire for America was born in my heart, and not because of the grandiose dreams my father had for me, but, rather, because I could not wait to meet her people. Those, I decided, would be *my* people. As a fourteen-year-old, when we studied American history in great detail from its inception up to the Civil Rights Movement, I reflected on that day in the car with my father, when the burning desire for America had been born. I dreamed of becoming a writer and philosopher (although I still had only read a few writings of some philosophers). And, then, one day, something happened as we were discussing the "one-drop" rule in America—a rule that does not apply in Jamaica. It is a rule that identifies anyone who has even one ancestor of sub-Saharan-African ancestry ("one drop of black blood") as black. I realized that the possibilities to accomplish those dreams my father had talked about, which were becoming my dreams, would be spread among various races of people. I began to realize that I could not ghettoize my existence by limiting my possibilities according to a racial index. I would take the very concept of race as irrelevant to my existence. If I did not—and I panicked at this thought—then most of the roads leading to possibilities would be foreclosed to me. Race, I decided in that American history class, would not hold me back. I would propel myself forward into a world of endless possibilities and conjoin my spirit to a nation of individuals who, like me, were on a road to infinite moral becoming. But, there was more to my musings than this. One of the best gifts bequeathed to me was from my father in the form of a journal. I have been keeping one ever since, storage units of the mind where I record not the journalistic minutiae of my life, but the ideas, convictions, perceptions, and analyses that form a unified system, a comprehensive sense of the world that I cleave to and find anchorage and roots to tether a life that makes me feel more comfortable in air than on earth.

In my journal, I wrote that I would choose this first country as a place to transplant my inner core. I began asking who I was at the core and found that I was an insatiable and voracious aspirational being, with a longing for a venturesome future. I wanted to become "other" than what I was. In my growing fealty to reason, in the honoring of my own intransigent individualism, and having witnessed how socialism had ruined Jamaica a few years earlier and was, in my adolescent mind, continuing to do so, I made a decision. I decided that unlike many stagnant nations in the world that I had studied, nations that had ossified into custom and tradition, America was an evolving entity, and, more importantly, I wrote, it responded to certain moral values cultivated in one's character. It was not a malevolent place. It would reward you if you held certain values that corresponded to its fundamental principles and values. It would reward hard work, resilience, tenacity, a formidable will, and a disciplined mind that could execute work and initiative.

It would be a wonderful adventure, I decided, and I'd never be lonely. This was my second incarnation. My third incarnation would occur on that afternoon my plane landed in Atlanta and I made the formal and sacred covenant with America, in an America that had already achieved its Third Founding.

What I want to say to you is that we each must create a philosophy for our lives, to both affirm our existence and to give us fuel in times of challenge and crisis. I came to America armed with such a philosophy, a rudimentary one about America that was rooted in my being and that insulated me against any incursions against my humanity I was ever likely to encounter. It is not the responsibility of society or of the state to furnish us with such a philosophy.

It must generate from a hunger within. That philosophy must cultivate an ethos and craft a self-made soul. I believe that from the depths of a soul longing for a better life, a life of community and belonging, that we can begin a lifelong process of creating a philosophy that can usher in the world we desire. It is a world in which we can love our fellow citizens regardless of race. Since this was the philosophy I had come armed with, it did not matter whom I met along the way, or who tried to obstruct my path as I sought to preserve my existence. My existence, buttressed by a life-affirming credo, would be inoculation and attractant simultaneously. My existence, unlike those who take themselves to be radicals in the United States, would never be articulated as a form of resistance or rebellion. To construct yourself as a negative is to negate love and the freedom and potentiality that reside in you. My existence has always been conceived as a universal conjoinment with others. This fluidity in existence is what I believe has allowed me to navigate so easily among so many different racial and ethnic groups, not just in America, but all over Asia, South America, and most of Europe where I have traveled and even lived for a while.

But, you see, this is already America, the universal first country you have created—a benevolent and welcoming non-xenophobic polity. It is a country where an Ethiopian cab driver can stop off at a local pub as so many do while driving me to some destination and have a beer and strike up a conversation with an average American. Many a driver has confessed such tales to me. It is a great nation where foreign accents arouse curiosity more often than they do hostility, and where differences in religious practices are not just protected by law, but are also enshrined by the respectful attitudes you have towards differing faiths.

Your valorization of the free market system has raised the standard of living for all, and, increasingly, brings the luxuries of modern life into the hands of the many, but it is more than that. You were the first people to understand the full and exact meaning that each person is a true end in himself or herself and not the means to anyone else's end. You made the trader principle an equalizing force in human relations, and that is why my friend Thai, in becoming a business property owner, could be the physical imprimatur of a moral axiom made possible by American capitalism: that private property is not a social convention or an institution created by government. Private property is a natural right required for human survival and happiness. I did not grow up with this realization. It was a discovery I had to make on my own.

My intellectual sensibilities were erected in a quasi-interregnum in the midst of a collapsing empire and the emergence of an independent nation. When my father was born, his father, a pioneer in the independence movement in Jamaica, was being held in a British concentration camp for being an insurgent and a hardline communist. From the stories my paternal grandmother has told me, he was tortured and beaten and no doubt also humiliated by the British. My grandfather, Frank Hill, was a first-class intellectual of the highest order, an aristocratic man of letters, and one slated to become Jamaica's first prime minister, an opportunity he quickly rejected by forming the first trade union for colored people and editing the Caribbean's largest newspaper, *The Gleaner*. He was an intellectual and educator before he was a politician. His black body, too, was a target for the abuse. I am, however, the legatee of a great tradition that he imparted. And, though I am certainly not a communist—just an old-fashioned conservative liberal—I did learn a few moral values through example from this toughest of giants. Resignation, aggrievement, and victimology were useless for those who intended to create their own destiny. If you had all intentions of creating a new nation and you fancied yourself one of its moral-political architects, you could not for one second believe that you had no power to liberate yourself by your own efforts! One was influenced by one's environment, but one was most emphatically not the product of one's environment. Without what Coates calls in his book a *specious hope*, one was a lifeless effigy, a mere pretense at life, a routinized wind-up doll with as much vitality as one is likely to find in a morgue. Grit, will, resilience, tenacity, reason, hope, dignity, perseverance, and an unflinching self-esteem that was earned through the virtues of your moral character gave you superlative self-confidence and trust in life's better possibilities. You never extricated yourself from the historical process because to do so was to become irrelevant to life; it was to drain yourself of all the creative endowments and capabilities you have for making yourself into a human being, the project of which is always ongoing.

Ideas were exchanged against the backdrop of tumultuous politics, states of emergency, roadblocks, and political arrests. They were used satirically among interlocutors who had been punished for their convictions to parody their persecutors and prosecutors. Although any among them could claim legitimate victimization, one would never know it, as their words delectably flowed from their lips amid a cacophony of raucous laughter. The air was laced with the smell of tobacco, aftershave, and the perfume of intellectual ladies dressed in pearls and satin frocks who elucidated their husbands' points and made better points of their own between long inhalations of cigarettes held in sleek silver and black holders. The air was also impregnated with the indelible smell of the sea, although from where we sat, only the infamous looming Blue Mountains that once shielded rebellious slaves who had escaped after murdering their masters could be seen, but not the sea. But a discussion of ideas and their unmistakable connection to human lives was always complemented with mouthfuls of steaming rice and peas cooked in coconut milk, fried sweet plantains, and crispy red snapper so soft it dissolved right there on your tongue as a thought came to mind. Oh, the commingled joys of eating and thinking: the food ministering to the mind and its thinking, the mind and its thinking aided by a satisfied palate. It never mattered whether it was the abstract formulations of Karl Marx, Sigmund Freud, Wole Soyinka, Julius Nyerere, John Maynard Keynes, Ludwig von Mises, Max Weber, the Founding Fathers of the United States, or a formal analysis of elocution that was under discussion. Ideas, deeply experienced in my body as a visceral human animal, were all too human for me.

And, so, I came to America knowing that contrary to what people had said about its unintellectual, and, more ominously, deeply anti-intellectual, status, that such was not the case. America was founded first and foremost in the realm of moral and political ideas. It is a commonsense, action-oriented intellectual nation. It has no place, and should have little use for, the purely abstract theorizer who cannot apply his or her life directly to your lives. What I have come to discover is that the biggest breach in this country is not between the rich and the poor, not even between blacks and whites, and not between the socioeconomic classes. The most egregious breach is one that makes all the ones mentioned above possible: It is between the people and the elitist intellectuals, most of whom are ensconced in the safe havens of today's morally bankrupt humanities and social science departments which preach not just hateful invectives against America, but hatred of this country for its virtues. That most of today's humanities and social science professors are self-styled radical Marxists, cultural Marxists, and alt-leftists is in and of itself no legal crime. However, there is a gigantic gulf between those anti-reality-spewing invectives coming from the enemies of America and of reason, freedom, individualism, and capitalism, and their failure to connect to an American way of life and you, the reality-oriented, well-grounded American people. That gulf is so marked an indication of perceptual psychosis that if ever there were good grounds for dismantling and restructuring today's humanities and social science departments—chief among them being the philosophy and literature departments—and firing most of the welfare scholars who preach such nonsense, none better could be found than in the hotbed of conceptual jostling among socially irrelevant and insignificant professors. Those professors make up language as they go along to create alternate realities because the real one out there in the outside world rightfully does not give a damn about their existence. And, yet, is it today's intellectuals who are foisting the worst racial identity politics on the minds of today's young people and engendering an environment in which race relations are and shall continue to become increasingly toxic unless the present intellectual and educational trends are reversed?

The basic core principles and foundational structures that keep the United States intact, the ones that provide our citizens with their civic personalities and national identities, are being annihilated not apocalyptically, but in thousands of daily scratches. This is happening in the revisionism that passes as correctives to past social ills but that end up denigrating those very principles that were themselves responsible for the amelioration and destruction of the social and political evils that dehumanize and denigrate human lives. Any nation has to be judged fundamentally not by the actors who betray the principles and laws that secure individuals' rights, but by the principles themselves that, overtime, restrain the outlaws—especially when that outlaw is the state—and who violate the rights of individuals. Affirmative action was a procedure the state undertook as a corrective against its sordid history of discrimination against blacks and women. As it was complicit in the most egregious discriminatory acts against women and blacks, the ethical argument for it was that the state had to install remedial measures to systemically and institutionally provide an antidote.

Today, that same argument must be made against the manifest destiny of the intellectuals running the humanities and social science departments in today's universities, where the mention of the term "Western civilization" is equated with racism and cultural superiority and pervasive oppression. The rapid *genderfication* of our classrooms in which gender pronouns are being eliminated and professors are threatening to fail students who refer to one another as male or female is an overt assault on heteronormativity as an invariable aspect of the biological world. Such phenomena are supported largely by the state, as are the multiplicity of hyphenated studies, such as Women's-, Black-, Chicano-, and all sundry programs that seek not only to balkanize the university but establish *knowledge apartheid*. Knowledge apartheid is the view that all fields of knowledge are self-referential and exist as closed systems. Hence, any attempt to make any connection between gender studies and biology or male contributions to the very systems of logic that must be employed in any of what we may term *off-site disciplines* is rejected as bourgeois, Western, class-based, white patriarchal oppressive structures that circumvent the "lived experiences" of its subject/victims. The intellectuals who teach in these disciplines, while not believing that, say, women's studies is inextricably linked to the Cartesian subject, or that biology can explain why a trans-man can never give birth to a child—that person is still, biologically-speaking, a chromosomal female—and seek a doctrinal purity from a disciplinary standpoint. Yet the ultimate goal of these *off-site disciplines* is to impose a particular type of sensibility and disciplinary sensitivity on the rest of society. The goal of such disciplines is not so much to educate as to radically resocialize society into a garish image of their ideals.

The manifest destiny of the humanities and social science professoriat is to have politicized knowledge supersede truth, objectivity, facts, and genuine learning.

There are many social ills taking place in the academy, but one crucial *manifest destiny* of the cognoscenti who rule its turf is the abolition of reason, rational argumentation, appeal to traditional canonical texts as evidence for objective truths about our world, and belief in an objective reality. Reason, outside of the analytic non-postmodern philosophers who are the last defenders of the indispensable faculty of human survival, is ridiculed, dismissed, and targeted as a Eurocentric creation that has been used to justify colonialism, slavery, and genocide of native peoples.

This point is worth lingering over. Ordinarily, the best way to fight an intellectual adversary is precisely through a contest of the rational faculties. The person with reality on her side and with the best relevant facts and strongest argument usually wins. But, today's scholars in the humanities are increasingly dispensing with argumentation while declaring vehemently via contorted fallacious argumentation that the modern form of argumentation is a white Western Eurocentric form of domination and linguistic imperialism that silences racial and gendered and ethnic minorities, and that it devalues and annihilates the "lived experiences" and epistemological standpoints of those marginalized by Eurocentric anachronisms—forms such as: evidence, facts, truth, objective reality, logic, and reason. Since one, in effect, cannot argue with such people, the only alternative, given the cognitive and epistemological harm they are inflicting on today's young people, the torturous breaking of their conceptual faculties, is to shut them down. To silence them by disarming them from their means of cognitive corruption. If and when they return to reason, logic, and a respect for rational argumentation, and renounce the untenability of their ethical relativism, then they can be allowed back into the pantheon of human educators. As one can have no truck or negotiation with terrorists, so one cannot reason with academic nihilists who have repudiated the sole dignified and only means of proper communication among human beings.

Identity politics, victimology, and multiculturalism have reached such astronomical heights in the university that not only are canonical texts being discarded, but trigger warnings are being issued in many universities for students who feel oppressed and traumatized that they have to read texts written by dead or white living men. These are men who are being read because they fundamentally changed the fields in which they worked, and, in many ways, altered the way we look at the world.

The problem with multiculturalism in the academy was that each of the competing new disciplines saw its own distinct canon of works as the final authority on truth, truth that had been suppressed or, at best, concealed by a rigid interpretation of truth. For far too long, went the reasoning, persons belonging to certain groups had been relegated outside the mainstream of proper ethical and intellectual deliberation. Not only were their histories denied, but they themselves were never full-fledged members of the human community. History had not only been unkind to them, but they and their identities had been refracted through distorted perceptual lenses. Seen as barbaric, less than human, and devoid of full or partial agency, they had been theorized out of human existence into a netherworld of phenomenal anomalies. Intellectual disciplines in the Western canon could never access their existential plight correctly, and nor could their advocates perceive them as they were. At the base of their operational premises lay an ethically problematic project: to systemically prevent cultural minorities (from gays and lesbians, to blacks and Native Americans) from radically modifying and upsetting the received wisdom about their natures.

Multiculturalism's complicity in this perpetuation of mythmaking, in cultural distinctiveness and in the commodification of identity, makes it synonymous with cultural, ethnic, and racial monism. It is synonymous with ethnic and racial monism because pluralism in general and cultural pluralism are forms of identity essentialism. Multiculturalism, therefore, is a form of group politics veiled as a very partial plea for the state to usher in the goals and aims of a particular people, or imagined peoples, in competition with other peoples. Hence, multiculturalism has lost its once honorable goal of advocacy, which was committed to achieving democratic citizenship and equal liberties among all groups to a guarantee that scripted group identities will survive over time. This survival over time will ensure the cultural authenticity of all persons who belong to distinct groups.

Multiculturalism is, therefore, bad for race relations.

Who is to blame?

It would take another book to discuss the root causes of how we got here. And, simple mono-causal explanations will not suffice. What will have to suffice is the state's willingness to allow a rampant version of identity politics and the vapid politicization of our educational system to destroy the backbone of American life that stands for reason and individualism. The balkanization will only get worse as progressive education continues to gain ascendancy in tertiary and higher education as each warring group vies for political pull and knowledge and learning becomes devalued in our post-truth society.

Who is to blame is the state for engaging in *educational cronyism*, for becoming ideological purveyors in a culture war, and for committing the worst crime, which is siding with the enemies of reason, capitalism, individualism, and Americanism, and giving employment to such destroyers of America. In other words, those who practice hate speech against America in the universities. It is difficult to describe this state of affairs in a few pages; however, after being a member of the academy for over twenty years, I cannot describe the degree of rampant anti-Americanism in today's universities, particularly within the humanities and social sciences.

The American professoriat hates America!

And, it spreads and indoctrinates that hatred among the college-educated young people in nuanced ways as politicized scholarship. The result is not just an educational crisis, but a national security crisis, as we are faced with a large percentage of students whose education is forged in the crucibles of a distorted view of what constitutes knowledge, an eroding commitment to the rigors of rational argumentation and logical inquiry, and an outright dismissal of their Western heritage. Let it be known that every person, regardless of race, ethnicity, or sexual orientation, who resides in the Western Hemisphere—including the current Native Americans living on reservations today—are the heirs of a Western identity.

But, let me return to the question of our educational crisis, which is becoming a national security threat. If the enemies of our great nation—primarily elitist welfare humanities and social science scholars in today's universities—are hijacking the minds of our students and infecting them with anti-Americanism, who will be left to defend America when the hordes of primeval barbarians who threaten us from outside descend upon us and destroy our unprecedented civilization? Who will defend the quintessential American values that have functioned as bulwarks against all sort of thuggish and destructive elements against Americanism—from within and without—and so unapologetically and proudly? The question we face, folks, is not who will be willing to die for America, but, rather, who will be willing to live for her consistently with dignity, implacability, and intransigent pride?

Who is it that provides the material resources, the financial aid, and who makes it possible for the haters of America, the destroyers of the minds of our young? The answer is that it is you, the silent minority, those who fund our universities in large proportions or even with small donations. You do so in the name of the best within you, in complete trust that our intellectuals in the universities will act in your own interest, speak in your name, and reflect your deepest beloved pro-American values. You have been wrong, and the time has come for you to stop funding your destroyers. It matters not whether you are a small-time, ten-dollar-a-year donor or a multimillion-dollar corporate grant funder. Reflect on the virtues of character that went into the earning of your money that, in innocent good faith, you give away to the bastions of higher learning, which are purveyors of a creed of vile hatred. Grit, honor, tenacity, discipline, old-fashioned honesty, and hard work are what you had to forge in your character to finance the cognitive debauchery of people who either think they are better than your crass materialism—without which they would be unemployed—or who think that you are complicit in an evil system (capitalism) which they are transcendent of, but which you, through your moral corruptness and complicity, force them to sink into the filthiest and inescapable murkiest depths.

Well, withdraw your support and leave them to fund themselves, to fester in their hatred of America and pit their wares on the free market, or on the subsidized floors of those public universities that your tax dollars are financing in totem. I have grown weary and plain disgusted as a patriot and lover of this great nation and admirer of the American people to see both dragged any lower into the muck of irrational condemnation for people who hate the goodness of America for no other reason than because it is a good and benevolent country. Their acts are sacrilegious because it stakes a stylized work of art that is America, and its magnificent systems, and reworks them into horrific tales of oppression, injustice, and indiscriminate biases. I say to you that whether you are an entrepreneur big or small, a day laborer, or a struggling professional, it is you who have made this country great. The only group of intellectuals who ever contributed anything of lasting value to the spirit of this country were the Founding Fathers of this nation. They were also the last of her intellectuals.

Americans, with their commonsense, everyday-applied logic in the material world, are who make America work, and they contribute more lasting value to the real philo-sophical nature of this country than all the professoriat in today's humanities and social science departments. Why? Because their political ideology of Marxism, anti-reason, and anti-capitalism—and, therefore, anti-individualism—is untenable and, *a fortiori*, their concomitant moral hygiene is misplaced in the clean and efficient and productive tech-nological civilization that you have created and that you maintain daily.

When the director of the humanities center of my own university can be allowed to host and proudly celebrate the 100th anniversary of the Russian Bolshevik Revolution, a revolution that ushered in the criminal era of Stalin, a political thug who personally authorized the deliberate star-vation deaths of millions of kulak peasants in Soviet Russia, the executions and imprisonments of millions of dissent-ers, and the communist enslavement of Eastern Europe, then there is no lower place to sink in terms of intellec-tual obfuscation of truth, honesty, and the willful display of contempt for the violation of basic human rights. That such an open celebration of such egregious evil is blatantly displayed without opposition is a sign of how much of a monopoly the alt-left intellectuals have in the universi-ties, and how much control they exercise over the minds of young Americans today. When the same humanities center ostentatiously declares time and time again its open contempt for objective scholarship, intellectual ideas, and pro-American values, denouncing the idea of seriousness itself in the pursuit of learning, then one realizes that it is today's universities that are destroying this country. As evidence, I offer you the actual flyer advertising for an obscene event from the humanities center at my university. Someone among the cowardly lot of today's professoriat must be a whistleblower and out the perverted obscenity that is passing as scholarship today: the moral degradation of intellectual values that has the infernal impertinence to charge students forty thousand dollars in tuition fees per year to attend the university at which I teach. The advertisement, in verbatim, reads as follows:

Are you dying to take a selfie with Zombie Shakespeare?

Are you interested in the real-life horrors of corn syrup, Confederate statues, mirrors, serial killers, "sexy" Halloween costumes, TED talks, and clowns?

Would you like to get a free tarot card reading by a real witch (who can also tell you about the history of misogyny related to witch-hunts and the horrors of the everyday patriarchy)?

Would you like to have on-demand horror-themed poetry written especially for you while you wait?

Do you have an interest in what the painting "American Gothic" would look like if it had a child, was turned into a movie directed by someone who considers David

Lynch tame, and slyly took up issues of neoliberalism, immigration, community, and loneliness all with an edge of noir gore?

Then join us on Monday, October 30, 2017 (6:00–9:00 p.m., DePaul Student Center, Room 120), as the DePaul Humanities Center proudly presents "The Horror of the Humanities V"!

*Our fifth annual Halloween event begins, as always, with an avant-garde "haunted house" (6:00–6:30 p.m.) featuring multimedia and interactive displays, installation art, and exhibits pointing to the **horror of everyday** life as well as the **relationship between horror and the history of the humanities**; continues with a screening of a contemporary masterpiece of Americana horror, The Eyes of My Mother (6:30–7:45 p.m.); and concludes with a talk and Q&A with the film's director, Nicolas Pesce (7:45–9:00 p.m.). Horrific surprises abound on Halloween Eve at the DHC! [DePaul Humanities Center]*

Please let us know if you are interested in bringing your class to this event, or in sending students on their own.

This is the state of the humanities and social sciences in today's leading universities. They are places where the burgeoning minds of young people are turned into miscarriages, where sites of learning are turned into inverted freak shows, and heroes of Western civilization are shorn of their greatness and made into maudlin caricatures. It is a place where students are taught to jeer and scorn before they can think and revere. Degradation and deformity of the human mind and arrestation of conceptual development are the goals of many of the professoriat in our humanities centers today.

The director of this humanities center in my university should be dismissed for student abuse and neglect. If he were to do the physical equivalent to students' bodies as he is doing to their minds, he would be imprisoned. But, even more than the body, our minds are our basic tool of survival, reason our only tool of cognition, and a guide to the choice of our values. Those who openly will the destruction of the mind, and who have the open institutional support, must be stopped by the most courageous among us, and in the name of the best within us.

The solution is not just to defund the American humanities and social science departments in current universities, but to also shut them down entirely and rebuild them from scratch.

* * *

Although I have a wonderful relationship with my students, I can see where this educational ethos is bad for white students and equally disastrous for black students. It colors ideas and makes the concept of a core common humanity that binds all Americans impossible. When I tell my urban black students that they have more in common with a white suburban student than they do with a Nigerian Ibo tribesman, I cannot describe the painful look of incredulity my declaration is met with. When I tell my white students that the founding of modern America black agency is inseparable from European constructs of identity, they spout some version of leftist Afrocentrism that they have gleaned from a carryover class they took in literature or sociology on the order that: *Blacks are in need of recovering their original ancestral beginnings that are devoid of white intrusion.* And, when I mention that their own American identities are deeply implicated in the history of black people, they seem nervous and revert to an appeal to their own symbolic ethnicities by telling me that they are 100 percent Greek or Italian or Polish—as if all those ancestral identities superseded and invalidated the most important one. That they are socialized bona fide Americans first and foremost. Why is being an unmediated American, plain and simple, such a shameful identity to hold?

The point is that so many of us have ceased feeling proud enough to simply refer to ourselves first and foremost—regardless of where we come from—as 100 percent American! Period. To declare that would entail embracing consciously all the values that go into making America the country that it is. To say I am an American, today, is not to appeal to some value-laden, amorphous, and necrotic assemblage of blood lineage and/or some appeal to ethnic or racial purity. Being an American has always meant steadfastly holding to specific values. And it is values—life-enhancing moral qualities we develop in our characters, which propel life forward and push our own lives into the forefront of our consciousness so we develop a sustained and intimate relationship with our moral lives which are responsible for keeping us alive as human beings. We are not alienated from our human nature precisely because we hold moral values. Those moral values are anchored by our commitment to an American system that protects them, that says nothing and no one can ever alienate us from our core. And, nothing can pull us as Americans, all of us holding differing beliefs and concepts of the good life, but united in our commitment to the sacred first civilization that allows us to remain connected as one nation. We remain connected by a very American maxim that announces the following: *Your personal beliefs may differ from mine, your conception of the good life you have carved out for yourself may be strange to me, but, so long as you respect my right to hold my life in my own name and do not violate my individual rights, and so long as you do not try to foist your values and conception of your notion of the good on me, then I will defend and uphold your right to hold your personal values in your personal name.*

This is the benevolent American way. It is the only way that a heterogeneous but common humanity can be forged in our great republic.

Fighting for My Moral Life in America

THE BATTLE FOR MY MORAL LIFE in America came at two pivotal moments that constituted a grand arc in my existence.

The first was when members of the academic alt-left tried to destroy my career out of what I believe was sheer envy, malice, and ideological resentment. The second was when I attempted to take my own life.

I fought both battles with all my heart and soul and won them. One was foisted on me; the other I undertook of my own volition. Since I have never been a victim, and will never be a victim in my lifetime, I claimed both as my personal responsibility to resolve so long as I chose life. In the end, I did choose life, and that has made all the difference. Here is that story:

I'm sitting in my office in early January of 2005. I've been sitting there for almost seven hours with my former partner. I'm awaiting the news of the vote of my tenure decision at the university where I've been teaching for five years. The meeting has been unusually long. The deliberation process in most tenure cases exceeds no more than two hours. I'm expecting the worse. My relationship with my colleagues has been cordial; however, I am a conservative liberal in a far-left, postmodern, Marxist-inflected department (we have a devotee of Mao, of all things, among our ranks who extols the virtues of the Cultural Revolution). What this means for me is not just that I am an outlier, but that, on some level, I have been a deeply resented figure in the midst of a collective whose philosophical and political viewpoints are diametrically opposed to mine. I am an advocate of reason, capitalism, rugged individualism, and self-reliance. I have been a trenchant critic of racial identity politics, multiculturalism, and illegal immigration, and the advocate of foundationalism and universal cosmopolitanism that, in effect, repudiates all forms of race-based claims to special entitlements. I have not been popular among the radical left-wing graduate student population, several of whom spend more time trying to abolish the prison system and advocate for the elimination of the police force than on their dissertations. But, above all, in 2005, I am an outspoken junior member of the department. I state my convictions politely but clearly. I am not an apologist for American exceptionalism among a denizen of people who claim to be very critical of America, but whom also resent the country enormously. When I hear capitalism being denounced, I respectfully, and with a smile on my face, explain why I think the denunciation is wrong and misguided. When a colleague openly advertises his admiration for the erstwhile, late Venezuelan thug President Hugo Chavez, I express dismay.

A colleague told me I was thought by some of my colleagues to be "uppity." I never cringed at the description. I made a mental note that the moniker was being directed at me by so-called progressives and chuckled at the irony and hypocrisy of it all.

I have been told by fellow colleagues that I should follow the hierarchy and keep my mouth shut at faculty meetings. I find this strange, given that these groups of individuals pay a great deal of lip service to being enemies of hierarchy and status. Nevertheless, I refuse to be bullied by anyone. I stand up for myself in meetings, and, though I do not have tenure, I defend my position as rationally as I can, and often express my dissatisfaction at the way academic life in general and the writings of academics who are so removed from the lives of ordinary Americans. I am told that some people think that by my attitude, I am something of a dilettante rather than a serious scholar. I already know, having completed a doctorate in philosophy, that to be considered a serious scholar in the American academy—at least in the humanities—one's work must be as far removed from the real world as possible and must be comprehensible to just a few specialists in one's field. This stamp of elitism rubs me the wrong way. Having been trained first as a political journalist in the harsh world of Jamaican culture, the sentiment leaves me deeply disturbed.

But, as I reflect in my office on the likelihood of my possible dismissal from the university, and, for all practical purposes, the end of my academic career—a career which I'd spent a lifetime preparing for—and, despite an excellent publication record, excellent teaching evaluations, and a stellar service record, was reminded of fourteen years earlier when I was shut out of graduate school for a year by the elite schools and the progressive liberals who ruled the roost because, as I was told by one of them, I was too committed to communicating ideas to the masses, and that I was just not pedigreed enough. The masses, one professor told me, were morons, and incapable of understanding philosophical ideas. This is the moral hypocrisy of the far-left. One professor at Emory University's philosophy department told me simply over the phone that my type was simply not welcomed in the department. I had graduated *magna cum laude* with an additional award as the most outstanding philosophy student of the year with competitive GRE scores; however, in my writing sample I had mentioned that I had often turned several of my philosophy papers as an undergraduate into newspaper editorials. This was both to communicate ideas to a broad readership, and to support myself during college. He had echoed the sentiments of another professor at Syracuse University, which had offered me a scholarship, and then retracted it upon learning of my deep desire to communicate ideas to a wide audience. This progressive professor regaled me with a barrage of insults. How dare I? And, who did I think I was, peddling my sophomoric ideas and high school opinions, and aspiring to elevate them to the level of human knowledge? Did I not know that I was nothing but a graduate from a second-rate state institution? And on and on, until the phone disappeared from my hands and I knelt to the floor, cringing in utter disbelief at the cruelty of people who took themselves to be agents of compassion.

Later that evening, as I shared the story with my mother, I remembered her kind words. "Every success story starts with a simple idea. Yours is just being born."

Every university I applied to the year I graduated from college with the highest awards and scholastic record turned me down. I went back to stuffing envelopes for minimum wages.

My mother's words reminded me of the covenant again, that sacred promise between myself and my adopted country made during that bumpy landing onto America soil years ago. My mother's words struck me as very quintessential American words. But, I "toughed it out" with American resilience and perseverance. The following year, I won a scholarship to pursue my PhD in philosophy at Purdue University.

The meeting for my tenure had started at 3 p.m. When my then chair of the department knocked on my office door at close to 11 p.m. to tell me the news was not good, I took a deep breath and moved into a field of opposition with strange equanimity.

The majority had voted not to grant me tenure. I was going to be fired from my job. I stood slack-jawed and resolute before her, with open palms extended towards the universe, and began the moral battle for my right to my life in America. It was the first moral battle I was forced to fight since coming to America. It was not to be a pleasant one. It would take every ounce of strength and resilience to withstand the unpleasantries in the ensuing months as the process made its ways through the various institutional channels. I went to my office, worked with my door open, greeted my colleagues amiably, taught my students, and resisted the litigious advances of lawyers eager to trade in on the racial implications of the case at hand. I would let my record speak for itself. I told my mother to pray for my adversaries, since, at the time, I was not particularly religious.

In the end, the battle was won. The university president, a huge fan of my work, granted me tenure.

I'd emerged from a battle with far-left liberals, some of whom exhibited the deepest form of racial animosity I had ever witnessed in America. And, here is what I'd learned. In this life, the chase for respectability at the betrayal of your own conscience leaves us all in the end unmoored to our deepest core selves. Perhaps we must stand alone, utterly alone in total abandonment from those whom we have believed were partners with us on a journey, so that when we reach the destination alone, we come to truly know the unalterable setting of our moral compass. Never again can we be abandoned. Never again can we lose our way. The desire for respectability is beguiling because what we aspire for is not validation of our values, but, rather, the simple visceral need for community and belonging at the expense of truth. In the process, we often disown and dissociate from our moral identities simply because, in the failure of others to recognize them, we feel alone.

Outspoken as I had been, I had, in some sense, traded my inviolable moral and political sovereignty for a sort of political safety net I had imagined these left-wingers would have given me if only I tried to advocate reason, appeal to a non-divisive universalism that I thought could unite humanity, and spoken a language of moral inclusiveness that I hoped could transcend all racial, ethnic, and national ties. I believed leftists in the academy were individualists. But, it was from them that I began to understand the true meaning of tribal collectivism and groupthink, of what herd and horde mentality looked like, and the price I would pay for deviating from the political script I was expected to adhere to as a fellow black progressive in the academy. Because I was never really a "black problem" to begin with, I had made their redemptive political calling null and void. The presence of what is perceived of as a black body, but one that does not exist as a burden or problem for others to solve, is an existential dilemma for left-wingers. It places them in an identity crisis, and the laws that govern their rescue fantasies are as invariable as the laws of nature in their own minds.

Steeped in their own racial and ethnic idiolects, they luxuriate in a porcine and somnolent deception that allows them to eschew self-examination in favor of exposing their own bigotry. Self-created moral popinjays who have been given a social dispensation, they and their victims of racial bigotry are transformed into certified moral icons. As progressives who accept their moral culpability in historical oppression, they can redeem themselves (in their own eyes), but you the victim need to be humbled and reduced by your oppression. When you declare that you are their equal, guilty as they are in the discriminatory transgressions of life, superior to them in many respects, and possessive of no more or no less of humanity in your agency, they see red flags. You can be a bit angered by it all—it reminds them of their own vitality and power to move the passions, but God help you if you declare that such progressives are mere social ballasts in your life, nuisances you'd just like to see get out of your way. They really don't matter. Never have. And never will. They'll crucify you because your indifference to the legitimacy of their self-appointment as sentinels of social justice and destroyers of systemic and institutional racisms is a sign of your deep ironic detachment borne out of observation. They are as complicit in structural racism as any self-declared bigot you're likely to encounter on the road to hell.

I won the moral battle when I accepted the strength that had always resided in me to stand alone and to simultaneously stand with God by my side and inside of me. I irresolutely learned to move the arms of my own moral compass solely by the dictates of my moral conscience. I won the battle when I reaffirmed the covenant and knew that the best among us is not an accident of mere hope, but consists in the constant will to rid ourselves of the lowest common denominator within us. The covenant with America was always my saving grace. I could not let her down. I could not betray the noblest within her people. I could not sacrifice the best within the civilization's principles and values. She had issued a clarion call to me on that first day I landed: "Come in. Come in."

* * *

In any story, there is always a personal component to a moral battle that is being waged in one's life. I would be remiss to state the case for my moral battle in America as one pitted in purely political terms and absolve myself of all personal stakes in a battle culled from within the darkest reaches of my soul. I have carried darkness in that soul while journeying into the light America has always shone in my presence: above my head, behind me, and illuminating my path ahead. Sometimes, however, a soul can turn dark and blot the light out—for just a while.

* * *

One night, some years ago, I downed a handful of pills, slowly. They felt like shattered pieces of glass piercing my parched throat as the bottle of wine I gulped in mouthfuls forced the shards to dislodge themselves from the thirsty membranes of my windpipe and reluctantly made their way deep, deep inside of me to settle somewhere between the space where reason and madness face off and simply cannot see where there is to get to.

On my back, hands clasped in prayer over my stomach, I felt myself easing into the dark hour. This farewell would not be a return to the womb—that claustrophobic and toxic wasteland where the embryo hears the cacophony of cries of lamentations and regrets over an accident too far gone to repair and is condemned to an eternal performance throughout its life. Death would be a conscious reversal of birth, a farewell that would be a homecoming, a return to one's self; this time, on one's own terms. Death would be easy. Clean and pure as the painless intrusion of a knife so sharp the flesh greets it in gratitude and falls away effortlessly.

The first time I had tried it at the age of seven, it had contained all the idiotic movements of an inexperienced neophyte—accompanied by the two fatal flaws in every would-be suicide's attempt: panic and mistrust of one's judgments. This time, easing into my bed with the solemnity of a calm assurance one has genuflecting before a crucifix in a cathedral for the first time, I felt myself slipping back to who I really was; to an authentic abstraction—pure will—sans the artifices of an illusory civilization that had tricked me into believing nature was on my side, and that I was something special. My death would not be a renunciation of the world or a repudiation of life. My personal denouement would not be elevated to the level of a metaphysical absolute worthy of universal contemplation. I simply wanted to return to my deepest self and to a curious state of complete inorganicity. This would not be a return to warm saline and slimy mulch, but an impersonal journey back into the asocial embrace of nature's arms.

Around 2 a.m., I felt myself slipping over to the other side—the moment when the heart rate slows interminably and will stop forever. My hands grew cold and wet. I began to perspire slightly around my temples. I was at peace. I saw the face of my mother looming over a coffin. I was inside that coffin. She was weeping endlessly. She was inconsolable. I saw my brother's face. It seemed distorted and twisted into a shapeless cartoon figure. I began to realize it was the ugliness of pain. I felt myself slipping some more.

Then I remembered the sacred covenant and my life. There was America. There was this world outside my apartment. It was a cold night. Wet and damp in Chicago. It was early May. I remembered the boy at twenty and the covenant he had made. I could think of no failing in all my years here it had suffered me. Trembling now all over, I reached for the phone by my bed and, with my eyes shut tight, and tears running down my face, I somehow dialed 911. They took me to the hospital. I told them what I had done.

And they took care of me.

I spent five days there.

When things are illuminated, life is beautiful. Luminosity is, indeed, a wonderful thing. You are anchored in your body, and that body is easy to please. You only have to honor the integrity of your senses. The bad smells bad, and the good is to be luxuriated in. You feel your senses acutely and realize you were blessed with them because they make you into a deep participant in life. Others have their senses too, and you share yours with them. Social intercourse is your way into earthly heaven. You are not alone.

Life belongs to you. Life can be shaped according to your vision and by the grace of its better possibilities. You love life and intend to affirm it by being a coauthor in the shaping of a destiny you have faith in: It can only be for your good.

Things are illuminated. Then, life comes crashing down.

I collapsed in my bathtub and the doctors said it was anxiety. But, I sensed it was more than that. During the next couple of months, I carried a constant Death Baby inside of me, one that dreams of and yearns for death. It felt as if I were being eaten from the inside out by this creature. But, still, I wrote. Poetry came flowing out of me like mineral water from hidden rocks. I'll spend months revising them. For one year it feels like I am drowning, but the poems just come pouring out. In spite of it all, I teach, think, and write and finish a new book.

Suicide seems like a good thing to think about. Suicide is calming. That's when I empty the pills in my hands one night and look at them for an hour. I contemplate them like little religious icons. Religious icons, though, belong on a shelf. I put them back in the bottle and line them up with my other bottled icons. They make a shrine I neurotically fetishize.

Suicide seems like a real possibility. I begin to think about it constantly. The pain is unbearable. I think, *How to do it?* I wonder, *Which way is home?*

Life is still on my side.

Bipolarism is the most lethal of all mental illnesses. It accounts for more suicides than the other illnesses and can catapult a person into the stratospheres of euphoria and then down into the darkest doldrums of depression and despair. When in the hypomanic phase, one can feel powerful; one can be extremely creative.

I hear this as a diagnosis as it is rattled off. It makes sense, I think. And, I begin to feel comforted. I am prescribed medication, and I begin to move once again in the world.

The poems keep coming, the sequel to my first book progresses, and I feel elation. Depression comes, but it does not last for very long. Then I begin to sink, deep, deep. I'm drowning and I can't breathe, and the vortex keeps swirling. I spend a few months staggering through life, often pacing the floors like a caged jaguar with too much energy.

Life is tired. Life becomes suspended. Life needs a break—from me!

Lithium carbonate—a salt—is used to treat, among other things, bipolar disorder. I am hopeful. I am relieved. Then it starts. The world becomes flat. I feel flat. I cannot feel. I am numb. My confidence is now erased from my soul. I cannot write. Words just won't come. Verbal creativity— once a constitutive feature of my identity—is gone. I stare at the screen; there are no words to fill even a quarter of it. In one year, there have been no new poems, although, thank God, I got one published in a good literary journal. All inspiration has gone; the vision behind the work is a blur, like the streaked makeup of an aging harridan. I am a harridan. Making love becomes a chore. The libido is a strange capacity I used to have but can't remember what it feels like. I cannot read. Dullness descends like some presage of gloom every time I attempt to tackle a book. My life was built around reading. That life is gone. My hand shakes constantly—the tremors—from the lithium. My face breaks out in acne and my back pushes out the assaults of this determined drug. I wait for the Second Coming, and it never comes.

I meditate on the covenant, but it seems so removed from my life. It is receding from my imagination. I sometimes reach out with my hands as if it is something I can just touch. I cry at times when I clench and then open my fists and retract my hands. When I open them, I am like a child—I expect to find something in them. There is nothing there. Still, I remember the boy who made the covenant. He must still live inside of me.

Months go by and I begin to feel a shift. My friend implores me to start blogging, but I balk at the idea. Blogs are for people who contaminate language. He persists. I begin and I am hooked. My creativity is improving. I begin to write a short story about my father's mental illness. I take a trip to teach a few seminars in Hungary, and ideas come pouring out—but just a few. I return and go to a conference and ideas are struggling to come forth slowly. I return to the writing of my book. Now, that's a miracle right there! I walk to the bookstore and buy a few books. In one sitting, I read eighty-seven pages. I begin to read several magazines cover to cover. Reading is a joy once more.

It is October. It's sunny and unbelievably warm for New York where I am visiting. I take a walk and feel my heart pounding, but it is not from anxiety. It is from excitement.

There has been a restoration—and a resurrection back to life. I skip along happily. I begin to wonder if it's legal to skip and to be happy. I walk aimlessly, entering a space that needs no name and no validation. I reenter life not as it ought to be, but as it is and always has been—waiting for me. Patiently. Lovingly. I think: I shall rise. I simply have to rise! I think of the covenant and I weep for its absence in my life. I cry because I had almost broken the promise it held in my life, and I cry over how close I came to crushing The Dream by my own hands. I cry because The Dream, that irreplaceable phenomenon of which I was the valued trustee and fiduciary, was almost annihilated by me. I cry because I know that in this great country I was privileged to live in, it is I who had the power to make that dream or to kill it. I could not know then that ten years later, owing to a proper diet, exercise, the recovery of a strong spiritual life and relationship to God, the continued cultivation of a formidable will, and the willpower to live a life committed to reason, that I would wean myself completely off lithium, and that the drug that had saved my life would be finally released from my life. I would be restored and brought back to myself.

* * *

I walk up Broadway and on to 120th Street and Riverside Drive, where I find Riverside Church. It is open. I do not absorb the beauty of the church. I am indifferent to its surroundings. I simply walk up the aisle and genuflect before the altar. I remember that I am in America. I remember that this is my country, where I belong. I reaffirm the covenant. I announce to God: *I am sorry for what I have done. This is my story. And, this is my life. And I want it back.*

Redemption, Hope, and the Declining Significance of Race in America

THIRTY YEARS AFTER BEING out of contact with Thai, we reconnect on Facebook. He's now fifty-two and a proud father of three daughters and three grandsons. He sold all three of his restaurants and moved to Los Angeles to be closer to his grandchildren. I chide him playfully in an instant message: "You mean you're rich enough to retire!" I announce.

On a whim, I decide to call him. I simply need to hear his voice. I'm shocked to hear the American twang in his accent. There is the sound of children's voices in the background. He tells me he's happy. He's had a good life. He taught himself how to trade in the stock market, and he made good money. He also flipped some houses in Florida during the real estate boom. He's had his failures too. Shortly after opening his first restaurant when I first met him, it had flopped within the first two years. He lost everything and had had to start all over again. But, in the spirit of a true uncomplaining American, he had started again from scratch. He and his young wife worked and saved and opened another restaurant in a more gentrified area, and it took off. In five years, they opened another, and three years later, they had a third. His father died before he was able to bring him over to the States, but he was happy his mother had lived to witness his success. He had brought her over a few years ago after his second grandson was born, and he was trying to teach her English—but she was stubborn. I told him to leave her alone, and we both laughed. I asked him how he felt about America. He grew quiet. The house actually seemed to grow quiet with the question, hauntingly so. Then he said in a soft voice:

"America has brought me where I am. I can't imagine a world without...you know...this place."

We chatted for a few more minutes as I filled him in on my life as a professor and book author. He asked for details. I told him that I had bigger dreams for my life, that that was the American way, but that, so far, I was proud of my achievements. After authoring three books on the topic of cosmopolitanism or world citizenship, from 2010–2012, a consortium of four universities in England held a series of conferences devoted to my specific theory of post-human cosmopolitanism and adopted the moral vision contained therein as part of their mission statements. They wanted their schools to be guided by the version of love for humanity I had been cultivating and advocating my entire life. Yes, I told him, my books in ethics and political theory are taught in college courses across the United States, and I had achieved full professorship in my mid-forties—long before I expected to do so. I'd given hundreds of invited lectures on my ideas all over Europe, Asia, and South America. I had led workshops on my books in the United States and Europe and China. I spoke at length about my love for humanity and my desire to unite all humankind through the propagation of my ideas on cosmopolitanism and love of humanity. The human species was the greatest phenomenon that could ever be contemplated. We had to see man as a majestic and heroic being; we had to judge human nature by the best of those who held the title of man. Thai grew quiet and then said he always remembered me going on about America when we were stuffing envelopes in the bank—that I had always said it was the greatest country on earth. Did I still think America was a great country?

"Of course!" I exclaimed. "Greater and nobler today than ever before. We must never give up on this magnificent and illustrious country."

Thai said he had always wanted to write something about his life, and I promised to tell a little bit of his story. He seemed happy. There ensued a long silence, and I felt joy in the silence. I realized that in our early friendship, because Thai spoke such little English, we'd often just sit beside each other in silence at lunch in the cafeteria—at least when I and our mutual friends were not "killing him with English," as we liked to phrase it. We'd just sit and sometimes look at each other and smile and not say anything and look out the window, and if the weather was nice, take a short walk. He often liked to look up at the sky.

The silence on the phone feels appropriate. Then I smile, and I know he is smiling back on the other side, and I tell him I'll let him get back to his family. But, he wants to talk some more. He asks me what I'm reading right now. I tell him the truth: that I've been amassing a bunch of articles on the improved nature of race relations in America. And then Thai tells me that he is married to a woman who is black. His parents had wanted him to marry locally, but shortly after I had gone off to graduate school, he met a woman who was a lot taller than he was, but whom he had loved at first sight. They met after he lost his restaurant. He was walking to the bank to pay an installment on his loan and, for some reason, he had gotten lost, and there she was, a beautiful black woman waiting to cross the street. She sensed he was lost and offered to help.

I'm rummaging through my files and articles.

"Thai, did you know that according to the latest Gallup poll conducted in 2013 that 87 percent of Americans approve of black/white marriages versus 4 percent in 1958? Did you know that approval rate for interracial marriage is now well over 90 percent?"

Thai laughs and reminds me he's not black. I tell him he's got a little "something" in him. He laughs hysterically. I tell him that a Pew Research Center study details a diversifying America where interracial unions and the mixed-race children they produce are challenging typical notions of race. Interracial marriages in 2012, I tell him, hit an all-time high. I tell Thai that *The Washington Post* found that America was among the least racist of nations in the world.

Thai explains that one of his daughters married a Puerto Rican, the other two married white men. His grandchildren look interesting, he says. They are on Facebook, he tells me. I just didn't recognize them as belonging to him!

A faint sadness overcomes me after my conversation with Thai. I begin to feel nostalgic, a strange nostalgia for an era that was different. Today, we live and work in an era of what we can call the Cult of Entitlement and the Cult of Trauma, a place where every slight experienced becomes a site of terminal injury and eviscerated dignity. I teach in an environment and live in a civilization where, increasingly, those who come to our shores illegally and legally are force-fed a diet of identity politics that encourages them to fight for rights of votership, endless public funds for education and healthcare, and basically estranges them from their country once they land here. Why does this sadden me? Why should I care?

There was something innocent in that struggle thirty-two years ago. There was the sense that America was a kind place. You could fail—though the thought was unspeakable to all of us. But, if you did, America would present alternative opportunities. Today, we are told America is a mean-spirited place, a country that stifles dreams, rides the backs of its minorities, and plunders them for profit. I hear the laughter of Thai's grandchildren, and I know in my heart we are cut from the same cloth—that he will teach them a different narrative. Here was a diminutive man barely five feet two inches tall, an impoverished peasant from Vietnam who had come to this country and saw not oppression and bigotry but a country whose streets were lined with sheaths of gold, and, barely able to speak the language, grafted himself into that nation and picked up a tiny piece of that gold for himself. And, you, my fellow Americans, you did not stop him. You shared the abundance with him as you knew you would when you created the laws that allowed him to be a part of your noble and great nation decades before. Such was the glory of your generosity and the glory you longed to see in the achievements of others. In those achievements, you saw paths to which you could aspire. You saw yourselves walking and conjoining yourselves among the strangers among us all, striving for unity in a common goal: to make something of our lives that we can each be proud of. Thai gave you and all of us that vision. A small-bodied man making great strides among us all.

I suddenly don't know what I'm doing, but I find myself rummaging through my files on race in America. It's good stuff. I want to send it to Thai. My eyes are filled with tears; I don't know why. I have no children of my own. I never will; perhaps that's why I'm on the verge of tears. In all the struggle to achieve, to write my books, to have overcome over two hundred rejections before I could secure a reputable publisher to publish my second book, I realize I will never have a son or daughter to whom I could tell that tale.

I begin to weep for that loss, for the absence and pain I feel in my heart, for the shortness of breath that constricts my breathing. I feel I need to send these articles on racial progress to Thai. I'll send them as links. But, in memory of an era in which we thrived as hopeful strugglers in a bountiful land as adventitious yearners, I'll send them as hard

163

copies in the mail. He should have them. His grandchildren are the legatees of an amazing American civilization that keeps getting better, that improves with age. They must never lose sight of that. They must never capitulate to that eldritch mythology that tells them America is doomed, that she is in an inevitable decline, and that she is evil. They must never be alienated from their rightful place in the pantheon of the greatest civilization in which they were born. They *are* the legatees of a great American civilization. I have nothing to give them but these articles that I can only hope will survive the test of time.

I implore and beg each of you, in the name of the best within you, make that civilization one that your children and Thai's children can be equal coparticipants in. Let there be no arbitrary dividers among your children and his children—and the children I would have had, had I been so blessed and privileged to have been a father.

Smiling and wiping back tears, I throw into the lot one of my books on love of humanity and what it means to be a human being in the 21st century, and I sign it with love for Thai and his family.

* * *

It's early fall, mid-October. Chicago. I've gone for a long bike ride, and I have parked my bike along the end of a long pier that juts out into the water of Lake Michigan. It's chilly and I'm underdressed. The sun was bright when I started out, but it has taken a brief sabbatical from warming the insides of others and is hiding deep, deep inside the reaches of the clouds I am peering up into the sky to see. A man, handsome, beefy, in his mid-forties, I suppose, and going bald with an accompanying receding hairline, stands at the end of the pier. He's teaching his son to fish. I observe from a distance as I park my bike and watch as he stands behind his son, towering gently over him, and shows him how to throw the line. I feel happy. I'm not sure why. No one else is around. The lake is smooth, no ripples after yesterday's heavy rainfall. The boy shouts. They've made a catch. It's a small perch. They lodge him in a large bucket. The man turns and, on seeing me, smiles, and the boy, around ten years old, jumps up and down in complete jubilation. I give them the thumbs up.

The man beckons with his head for me to come over.

I'm wedged between him and his son. He smells of cigarette smoke and cologne. I guess his accent correctly. Polish. His son high-fives me. I'm no good at this, I tell the man, who introduces himself as Mario. I throw the line. We wait. Nothing happens. I throw again. Again. Nothing. I offer the boy the line. He refuses, telling me it's my turn. I begin to shiver a little and the man picks up a large overcoat lying on the ground and wordlessly puts it over my shoulders. I say, "Thank you." We wait. I think I've snagged something. The bait is lost. Mario rebaits the hook for me and I throw the line once more.

I feel the tug. The boy senses it. Mario smiles. The boy begins to yell and jump excitedly. Mario lights a cigarette as I reel the catch in. It's a decent-sized perch.

"Wow, it's bigger than mine," the boy exclaims, as I dehook the fish carefully and place it in the bucket. Mario laughs at me as I sniff at my hands.

We're sitting now, huddled together at the end of the pier. The lonely sun has come out from hiding. It is time for her to go down. The buttery expanse of her glow is receding. We're all a bit chilly, I can tell, and pressing into one another unconsciously for simple warmth. Behind us, there is spluttering in the bucket. The boy says we should release the fish back into the lake. Mario shrugs, inhales deeply on the cigarette, and the two of them gently ease the fish back into the lake.

We're standing, looking at the setting sun. Quietly. We have not spoken much. Mario lights another cigarette and I feel both their shoulders touching mine. I could eat the whole world like an orange. I could turn to Mario and ask him, "Why are we are here and who is responsible?" I could hug his son and cry again at the loss for the one I never had. But, between the world and me stands two magnificent possibilities—right here, right now. Living and breathing in this moment. Two inviolable, *sui generis,* beautiful souls. They are what I have right now to hold onto until I go back home. They are benevolent gifts from God, standing in this wonderful place and time.

I look at the last resplendent glow of the setting sun and just place my arms around their shoulders and close my eyes and listen, listen to the sound of bare existence and feel the cadence of life coursing its way through my entire body. I open my eyes and stare over the lustrous expanse of the lake. I see a collage of all the immigrants, and my fellow Americans alike. I say a silent prayer for all of us. The world we desired has been won. It exists. It is real. It is possible. It is ours, my fellow Americans. I squeeze the shoulders of my companions and sense an endless connection of dots emanating between me and them and the world beyond us. I feel a deep sense of love in my heart.

I cannot, and need not, explain it.

I feel no fear in this moment, only a sweet desire to move deeper into this world I am in love with as the universe slides lovingly along my side.

Acknowledgments

A great many people contributed to this book, in large and in small ways. In particular I would like to thank Abe Greenwald at *Commentary* magazine for publishing an article in that magazine that inspired the writing of this book. My deepest appreciation goes out to David Bernstein, my editor at Bombardier Books. His enthusiasm and encouragement for this project are exactly what every writer dreams of receiving from his editor. My appreciation extends to the entire team at Bombardier Books/Post Hill Press for making this project possible.

The following people provided the unconditional love and support in my life that enabled me to write this book indefatigably and with implacable confidence: my mother; T. Nevada Powe; John Horton; Jose Gonzales; Mary Amico; Jonathan Diaz; James Ciccotti; and especially—Ray Richmond.

Shelby Steele's profound books on race relations have influenced my own perceptions of the meaning of race in America. I owe an intellectual debt to the late Ayn Rand whose philosophy gave me a comprehensive and integrated approach to philosophy and thinking. It was from her that I learned the importance of the absolutism of reason. Condoleezza Rice's writings have done much to shape my overall worldview of international politics, and her patriotism, dignity, and elegance as a human being in this world have been a source of personal inspiration to me.

About the Author

Jason D. Hill is professor of Philosophy at DePaul University and the author of three previous books, including *Becoming a Cosmopolitan: What It Means to Be a Human Being in the New Millennium*, and *Civil Disobedience and the Politics of Identity: When We Should Not Get Along*. He is also President and CEO of the Institute for Immigrant Assimilation.